Rock-Solid
Marriage

ROCK-SOLID MARRIAGE

Robert & Rosemary Barnes

WORD PUBLISHING

Dallas · London · Vancouver · Melbourne

Scripture quotations marked NIV are from The Holy Bible, New International Version. Copyright © 1973, 1978, 1984, International Bible Society. Used by permission of Zondervan Bible Publishers.

Scripture quotations marked KJV are from the King James Version of the Bible.

Library of Congress Cataloging-in-Publication Data:

Barnes, Robert G., 1947–
    Rock-Solid Marriage / Robert G.
  Barnes and Rosemary J. Barnes.
      p.   cm.
    ISBN 0–8499–3510–5
    1. Marriage.   2. Communication in marriage.
  I. Barnes, Rosemary J., 1949–   . II. Title.
  HQ734.B249   1993
  646.7'8—dc20   93—7083
                                                       CIP

3 4 5 6 9   LB   9 8 7 6 5 4 3

Printed in the United States of America.

Contents

Acknowledgments   7

Introduction   9

Part 1
Entering Marriage with Great Expectations

1 A Strong Foundation   13
2 Entering Marriage with the Wrong Expectations   22
3 Bilingual Marriage   32

Part 2
Choose to Be Married

4 Opposites Attract   43
5 Choosing to Be Friends   51
6 Attributes of a Friend   58
7 What About Fun? Remember Fun?   68
8 That's How Mom and Dad Did It   75
9 The New In-law Factor   85

Part 3
The Communication Process

10 Now How Could That Hurt Her Feelings?   95
11 Procedure Setting   107
12 The Listening Ear   115
13 But He Refuses to Talk to Me   123

Part 4
The Exercise of Conflicts

14 Conflict Aversion   131
15 The Conflict of Finances   143
16 Lovemaking from a Woman's Perspective   153
17 Sex from a Man's Perspective   161
18 Sexual Issues Spouses Sometimes Argue About   171

Part 5
Get Aggressive

19 Goal Setting   183
20 Your Spouse's Self-Esteem   192
21 Practice Safe Marriage: Use Protection   201
22 Third-Party Intervention   209

Part 6
It's a Matter of Doing Love

23 Love vs. Feelings   219
24 Deciding to Forgive   226
25 What Is Love?   236

Acknowledgments

There are a great many people who have played a part in helping to make this book possible, particularly the staff at Sheridan House who play a part in everything we do. Working with them every day is certainly a very encouraging ministry. We are very grateful to Lillian, Carol, Nancy, Duane, and Bob for freeing us to be able to write this book together.

The place we used when we began to write this book was like a dream, and we are very grateful to Fred and Lyn Hunter for sending us to their cabin. It was a wonderful place to write, to talk, and to be together as a family.

We are grateful to the many friends that God has surrounded us with, but our gratitude and daily prayers will forever remain with our two wonderful children Torrey and Robey. They have been a consistent blessing, and we pray that God will grant them a marriage and children that will bring them the same happiness that we have been blessed with.

Introduction

While writing much of this book we were spending three weeks at a friend's cabin in North Carolina. It's a beautiful home that sits on the side of a mountain. In fact, it looks very precarious the way it's perched. The front half is secured to the mountain, while the back half balances on diagonal stilts over a canyon.

To look at the cabin from the side one would think that it would slide down the hill if anybody had the nerve to jump up and down inside this building. But looks can be deceiving. It's as solid as a rock and has been for many years. That's because the designer did his homework before it was built. He anticipated the stress exerted because of the way the building hangs over the edge and designed a structure that would be able to withstand that stress.

That's why we have written this book. Over the past decade the two of us have traveled across North America presenting marriage seminars. We have been distressed at the lack of information that couples have about the basics of building a strong marriage.

All marriages spend some time hanging out over the edge. Entering into a marriage relationship without knowledge of some of the necessary principles can be disastrous. To make matters worse, today's society is not friendly toward the kind of commitment that a marriage requires. A lack of understanding of the foundational principles that make a marriage work can leave a couple vulnerable to a major "mud slide." May God bless your marriage as you read this "architectural manual," whether you have been married a few weeks, a few decades, or are anticipating marriage.

There are many ways this book can be used to help build a stronger marriage relationship. One way, and perhaps the best, is for a husband and wife to read this book together, out loud. Read one chapter a week and then discuss the questions at the end of each chapter.

A second way this book can be helpful is to use it in group discussion. Several couples can gather together, read the chapter, and discuss the questions. It is always helpful for one couple to hear that other couples have the same concerns and questions. It is also helpful for a husband to hear that wives, other than his own, have many of the same feelings.

This book can also be helpful as a study guide for those who are about to get married. It will stimulate conversation concerning different attitudes about the marriage relationship.

However this book is used, whether read by an individual or as a couple, it is our prayer that God will use it to bless your home.

Bob and Rosemary Barnes

Part 1

Entering Marriage with
Great Expectations

1

A Strong Foundation

Why does it seem so difficult for people to stay married these days? Why are people waiting longer and longer before they marry? Why are people choosing to live together before marriage, even though those who cohabit before marriage have a higher divorce rate? The real question to be asked is, "What is marriage anyway?" We have been surrounded by married people, from our parents and grandparents to the people down the street; unfortunately, we are seldom given a clear diagram of how to succeed at marriage, how to be successful at this relationship that encompasses the vast majority of our lives.

In 1988 we began to build a new counseling center at Sheridan House Family Ministries. Before we could actually begin building, the engineers took soil borings from the construction site. I assumed it was just a matter of formality, that they always went down deep into the earth beneath the proposed building to take soil borings. Then they would go on with the business of pouring the foundation.

When the results were completed, our general contractor and architect called to say, "We need to talk." Our contractor, Hugh, walked in and began, "Bob, I've got some bad news. The density of the soil is not strong enough to support the kind of building that we are going to build here. We'll have to sink pilings into the ground before we can pour a foundation."

They looked so serious as they talked that I knew pilings must be a significant undertaking. "What does that mean?"

was all I knew to ask. "It means we're going to have to pound concrete cylinders into the ground every six feet around the circumference of the building."

"Is that absolutely necessary?" I asked as my mind conjured up a huge price tag and weeks of delay. It was really hard for me to get interested in spending so much time and money on something that would be buried in the ground. No one would ever be able to see it.

Anticipating my response, Hugh said, "Bob, remember the problems we've been having with your first building. It was built back during the days when we didn't know enough to check the strength of the ground we were building on. That's why we have so many problems with the building sinking and cracking. The foundation is just not strong enough to handle the pressure."

The Ground We Marry On

Times may have gotten better for the construction industry, but that certainly can't be said for marriage. In days gone by, marriage was built on a strong foundation. Young people grew up in an environment that prepared them for marriage. In years past, they practiced in-depth relationships long before marriage. People grew up in a community and developed strong friendships with people of both genders.

Today's adult has generally grown up in several different neighborhoods. Statistics tell us we move every three to five years. As a result of this mobility, families are significantly more isolated than they were when generations of families grew up and lived in the same area. Today's neighborhoods even look different. Instead of building friendships, we now tend to build fences around our houses.

An example of this struck home last summer when we visited friends in a small Tennessee town. We were surprised to discover that even though our friends had lived in the town for two years, they still had only one other couple they consider friends. In fact, they had only been in one other house in their neighborhood. If this happens in a small town in Tennessee, imagine how much more isolated are families in other, larger communities.

Several factors contribute to this isolation in today's society. First, the soaring crime rate has made many people afraid to venture out of the security of their homes. Second, we have overwhelmingly busy schedules; we are too active to develop meaningful relationships. With both spouses working and the after-hours work that still needs to be done at home, families have time for very few activities together. And, of course, our culture is much more transient.

Put all these things together and it is easy to see that many people today grow up without having had the privilege of several deep friendships. Not having as much opportunity to practice having friendships and quality, long-term relationships makes it difficult for young people to marry and work out their new relationship. The foundational principles have not been taught. Young people are just not prepared.

No Rock of Commitment

An understanding of the concept of commitment is another ingredient necessary to build the foundation of a strong marriage. Commitment is something that is "caught" as much as it is taught. A child grows up and sees the commitment his parents have to the important things in life. Things like country, family, and God. His parents don't tell him these things every day. Instead, he sees his parents being active in civic affairs. He hears his parents speaking positively about the country. And he watches as his parents stand up to be counted on issues they feel are important. That's commitment at work for a young person to watch and catch.

That's what the child of yesterday was able to observe while growing up. But for the past three or more generations, we have pulled away from a society built around the family. In those earlier days children grew up in homes that put the needs of the family before the needs of the individual.

Mom and Dad sacrificed for the sake of the family's needs. In fact, it was very likely that the parents even worked together in a family-run business—a farm, a general store, or some other business with the home attached. The concept of sacrificing individual rights for the rest of the family's needs was built into everyday life. A child in that environment grew into adulthood watching and participating in a strong commitment to the family.

When you grow up practicing the concept of commitment to others, it's much easier to understand the need to commit and sacrifice for the sake of the marriage. Yesterday's child grew up in that family-centered society. Today's child grows up in a society that places great emphasis on the individual and his rights. Yesterday's child was taught to pursue meeting the needs of the ones he loved. Today's child grows up and learns to say, "She's just not meeting my needs anymore, so I don't think I love her."

It's this foundational principle of commitment that is missing from the background of today's child. He grows up thinking as an individual with lots of needs to be met, rather than as an integral part of a whole with the understanding of striving to meet another person's needs. The marriage suffers because of this preoccupation with individual rights and needs.

Erosion by the Media

There was a time when the media, as a form of entertainment, upheld traditional family values. Laugh as one might at Ozzie and Harriet, it was not a destructive force to the family as an institution. The media turned a corner when they decided to focus on making the marriage relationship look ridiculous and archaic while glamorizing extramarital affairs.

We are told that the average child watches between three and six hours of television each day. This is a new kind of television, where one grows up seeing the family denigrated as an unnecessary institution. After hours and years of media blitz that saturates young people with soap operas and sitcoms portraying that the most significant reason for a cross-gender relationship is sexual bliss, in or out of wedlock, it eventually becomes part of their thought processes.

The entertainment industry, the music industry, and news media that are obsessed with reporting about the marriages that fail, are eventually going to have an impact. Soon, perhaps even now, youngsters will grow up in this society with the subliminal suggestion that marriage is not really for keeps. If the marriage doesn't "feel good," walk away from it.

The foundation is further eroded by this barrage of images in our living rooms that entertain while suggesting that we are here to have fun. That attitude creeps into other parts of our lives, too. We get married with the thought that if it isn't fun, there will be someone else out there who can make it that way. Of course, we don't think in those words when we are getting married, but it's part of our culture's thought process. A newspaper on the West Coast ran this ad: "Wedding Rings for Annual Lease." I guess wedding rings are very expensive, so it might make more sense to lease them rather than buy them. That way, if things don't work out, you haven't wasted your money. Growing up in the last fifty years meant growing up in the era of the individual. Commitment to others went out the window.

The Erosion of the Last Pillar

Fifty years ago a young person's parents were the most influential force in their lives. Today a new force has taken over as the most significant power of influence. Parents are no longer on the top of the list. In fact, parents aren't even second. Television is the most influential power in a young person's life, and peers are the second. It's a battle between music and the parents for third place.

With the fall of traditional family values in our society and the rise of the power of television, a young person's parents are his last hope for learning the Judeo-Christian concept of marriage. Most of what we learn about marriage comes from the "laboratory" at home. We watch our parents and gain an understanding of what marriage is all about.

Parents influence our marriages in two ways. First, they model the marriage so we can watch it. Then, as we get older, they take time to talk to us about marriage; they prepare us.

In today's society, a young person stands just as good a chance of growing up with multiple parents, such as step-parents, as he does of growing up in a home with both parents. This makes it very difficult for a child to watch his parents model a marriage. But even in homes where a child lives with both his parents, today's dual-income, highly transient lifestyle has made it difficult for a young person to see his parents together at all. When they both return home from work, they race out the door in different directions to get the children to music lessons or dance lessons or ball practice, or get themselves to church or civic meetings. A person growing up in today's home doesn't get to see much interaction when a typical conversation consists of, "Who's going to pick up Johnny from the ball field, you or I?"

If the role modeling is bad, the lessons and discussions are worse. Parents today seem to be convinced that they should spend more time getting their children to soccer than talking to them about things that will really help them in life. Hence, a twenty-two-year-old gets married having learned how to compete in this world, but without the foggiest idea of how to relate to a spouse.

There's very little role modeling going on and even less time discussing how to relate in marriage. Parents just don't sit down and talk to their children and young people about the beauty and work involved in a quality marriage relationship, yet they expect them to marry and figure out this "lifetime commitment—'til death do us part" stuff. Today's couple is expected to build a marriage with no foundation whatsoever.

When Help Is Needed

Several years ago a friend of mine noticed that a corner of his house seemed to be sinking. This is not an altogether unusual happening in South Florida. With today's technology, he was able to repair this problem by pumping something under the weak foundation to avert disaster.

When the foundation of the marriage is weak and problems begin to develop, as they do in all marriages, where does one go for help? To a neighbor who is probably a stranger? To parents and other relatives who live in another state or don't have any answers themselves?

Today's couples can become so isolated that they have nowhere to turn for marital advice. They can also become so busy that they forget about working on their marriage. Then, with no foundation to build on, there are bound to be problems in the marriage today.

It's time to sit down and take a look at the marriage relationship. Society has left us on sinking sand, trying to balance a career, marriage, children, and outside responsibilities, all with blissful smiles on our faces. Then, when we find ourselves unhappy, we feel all alone and are left to believe that a change of venue, or partners, will bring us the happiness we are seeking. The incredibly high divorce rate for second marriages should show us that this is a waste of time.

It's not a new partner that we need. It's a new understanding of the marriage process. Just how does one stay married? The plain, square, gray foundation of a building is always there holding up the structure. There might be a fabulous ribbon-cutting ceremony with music, food, and dignitaries, but that's not what keeps the building on firm ground. It's the foundation.

So often we are led to believe that the marriage ceremony does it all. Once the wedding has taken place, then that's all there is to being married. "Well, now we're married," a couple might think. Nothing could be further from the truth. The wedding is a vow, a beginning, not a marriage. The vow is before God and witnesses, but the marriage is something that spouses must work at every day of their lives. It's a commitment toward another person's happiness and a move away from society's blast at the traditional family. It's a commitment to decide to learn more about another person and marriage in general, even though it wasn't taught at home. In other words it's a decision not to use "lack of a proper foundation" as an excuse not to build a strong marriage.

This commitment will cause a marriage to flourish. The information is available and so is the help. Though most of us go into marriage without any idea of what to do to stay married, that's no excuse. We can all learn if we want to.

When we started to build our new counseling center, I didn't know that the soil wasn't going to hold the new structure. That was no excuse. Today there are ways to find out these things. and it wasn't too late. I could still decide to take the extra time and expense to pound in the pilings and ensure that the building will be here long after I am gone.

Likewise, it may take an investment of extra time to examine the foundational principles of a marriage, even if the ceremony has already taken place. The rewards, however, are great, and they could have an impact long after you are gone. A marriage built on a strong foundation may influence generations to come. What could be more valuable than that?

Summary

1. Couples have a harder time working through the marriage relationship than ever before because they have no foundation to build on.

2. Often, people grow up in families that have moved frequently. They may not have had much opportunity to build strong friendships. This lack of experience with the relationship process makes it more difficult to establish a marriage relationship.

3. Today's society fosters a strong commitment to individual rights. Yesterday's society was built around a commitment to the family. It's more difficult to understand the need to commit to marriage when you have been raised to meet your own needs first. Commitment to something other than self is not taught in today's culture, and this has had an impact on the marriage.

4. The media and its constant attack on the traditional family has had an impact on what this generation believes marriage is all about.

5. Parents used to play the most significant role in training young people about marriage. Parents no longer fulfill this educational need.

6. When marital help is needed, today's couple is more isolated than couples were in the past.

7. A foundation can be established even after the marriage has taken place.

Discussion Questions

1. What has surprised you most about marriage?

2. What has surprised you most about your spouse?

3. What area of the marriage do you feel most uninformed about or unprepared for?

4. What has been the most frustrating aspect about marriage?

5. What has been the most difficult aspect about marriage?

6. What has been the most rewarding aspect about marriage?

7. Are you ready to make the commitment to build or repair the foundation of your marriage? Tell your spouse.

2

Entering Marriage with the Wrong Expectations

*P*eople are their own worst enemies when it comes to buying cars," my friend Bill Kelley said as we stood in one of the lots of Kelley Chevrolet. We were discussing the way people buy cars as we waited for another friend to go out to lunch with us. I had asked about the psychology of selling cars.

"There are several kinds of buyers," Bill continued, "but the most ignorant buyers are those who come to the dealer determined to buy a specific car. You can tell them about the car, they can ask questions and get negative answers. It doesn't seem to matter, they just want the car. You know in your heart that they'll be unhappy with the car in a few weeks. By their questions it's obvious to the objective observer that it's just not the right car for them. But they are determined to have that car. The younger they are, the worse they are. For some reason they overlook the negatives. They have certain expectations. Expectations can be very powerful deceivers."

Bill's observations can be applied to marriage, too. Several years ago John and Lindy came to the Sheridan House Counseling Center for premarital counseling. They were about three months away from their wedding, and the excitement was all over them. They each had fantastic expectations. The only problem was their expectations about marriage were not at all similar or realistic.

Her Expectations

Lindy expected the marriage to be an instant relationship. She and John would now spend the rest of their lives sitting or walking or just being together, having incredible talks. It was going to be a lifetime of friendship that grew deeper every day. Never again would they have to cut short their nighttime conversations just because John had to go back to his dorm. They would be able to talk forever.

Their lovemaking was going to be great because it would take place after these long, in-depth conversations. Year after year they would take care of each other. They would become one in heart, mind, and, oh yes, body.

Lindy, like many young women, anticipated a relationship that would continually grow. In her life with John she saw romance, sharing, intimacy, his mature leadership, and the security of the two of them planning for their future. She expected a partnership.

His Expectations

John saw the marriage as another step in his life. This was all part of the normal passage into adulthood. "It's like, you get your education, and then it's time to get married," John said. The counselor looked over to Lindy to see if she caught the magnitude of his statement.

To her it was a relationship. To John it was the next logical stage of growth. Now he would have a sexual partner as he began what he had spent years preparing for—his career.

The counselor summed up their different look at marriage for them. "Lindy," the counselor began, "you seem to view this marriage as a lifetime walk up a beautiful mountain. Constantly climbing higher, you seem to see it as an opportunity for the two of you to have a wonderful time working your way up this mountain called marriage relationship. For you the wedding is

just the day you arrive at the foot of the mountain and begin
your exciting trek.

"John," the counselor continued, looking at the young
man, "you sound like you see the wedding as the final arrival of
the relationship. Several times you have said, 'I really don't see
why we need to discuss all these different things. Once we get
past this wedding everything will be okay.'"

It was the counselor's recommendation that this couple
postpone the wedding for a few more months or, at the very
least, decide to get more serious about premarital counseling. It
was obvious they had very different expectations about marriage. But, as in the story of the person purchasing the wrong
car that Bill Kelley told, Linda and John were not to be de-
terred. They stopped the premarital counseling because they
felt it was only causing them to get off track.

Three years later Lindy returned to the counselor's office. "It's like our marriage never got off the ground," Lindy
began, tears streaming down her face. "We've been married
for three years, but we hardly know each other. Remember
that story you told us about the mountain and what I thought
about marriage. I've never forgotten it. I feel like John got
married and pitched a tent at the foot of that mountain never
to go any further. That's all he seems to want. I keep trying to
climb the mountain and call to him, but he's not interested in
climbing to a deeper relationship than we had on our wedding
day. As long as the sex is still there he seems satisfied." Then
Lindy finished with, "This is not at all what I expected marriage would be like!"

Causes for Expectations

"This is not at all what I expected marriage to be like."
What made Lindy think these things? What made her have
these expectations that she and John were instantly going to
become the perfect team? Where do expectations come
from?

Expectations are accumulated over a period of years by collecting data. Each of us receives input on marriage from various sources, and we file it away. There are several basic sources for these expectations: previous observations, previous experiences, and previous fantasies.

Previous Observations

Almost everyone has had the opportunity to observe some segment of a marriage. It is from those observations that we form our own expectations. We respond to these observations in many different ways.

Some children grow up in homes where they see very little marital interaction. The parents spend very little time together, or when they do it's behind closed doors. Other people grow up in homes where the adage is, "Never argue in front of the children." If these parents have disagreements, they wait until they are away from observers. Thus the children rarely see them disagree. It is only logical for the children from this home to assume that spouses who really love each other never disagree.

These are obviously very dangerous premises to take into a marriage. A day or so after the wedding takes place and the first disagreement erupts, the spouse who grew up in a home like those mentioned above has no way to compute a resolution to this disagreement. He or she didn't think lovers ever disagreed.

Every person must decide what to do with the information received from his or her parents' marriage. Some try to emulate the marriage without realizing that they don't have all the facts. They don't realize their parents really did disagree; the children just didn't get to watch the process.

Others will remember what they saw and attempt to do just the opposite. John saw his parents scream a lot. It was pandemonium in his house. The only way people got their point across was through loud outbursts of temper. He vowed that when he grew up and got married he would never yell at his wife the way his dad yelled at his mom. His home was going to be different. It's the right attitude, but it's more easily said than done. Unfortunately, when John became frustrated or tense he was prone to respond in the way he had seen things done in the past. It takes a lot of effort to overcome a previous "film" that has been run over and over in front of us.

One spouse had expectations of never disagreeing with her new spouse. Quiet tranquility was the atmosphere she anticipated. That was what she thought she saw at home, whether it was the real story or not. Of course, previous experiences did not tell the whole story.

The other spouse had expectations of never yelling or screaming at his wife. He had seen it done and vowed he never would do it himself. An admirable goal, but the observations of childhood are often difficult to overturn.

The previous observations built from these two homes couldn't be more different. Yet both persons had expectations, and both were devastated when their expectations weren't met. Lindy went into shock when John ranted and raved during the first month of their marriage. She had never had anyone talk to her like that. And she had never seen a husband talk to a wife that way. This was a traumatic experience for her.

John, on the other hand, knew that yelling wasn't what he wanted to do, and he knew it was wrong. But it really didn't seem that outrageous to him. "I can't believe she gets so upset. My mother didn't go into a coma when my dad raised his voice."

"Not only did he yell at me," Lindy said, weeping, "but then he couldn't believe that I didn't want to make love that night." Once again, she all but said, "This is not what I expected."

John then made a statement that showed just how far apart the two of them really were. "Lindy, I really don't see how the two are connected. How can the fact that I raise my voice one little time in an evening make it so you don't want to have sex?"

One was raised to expect the marriage to be a growing, developing relationship. The other got married expecting just simply to be married.

Previous Experience

Three years ago, when John and Lindy came in for premarital counseling, the counselor talked to them about their unrealistic expectations and the fact that they came from very different homes. They just listened and sat there smiling. It was as if they appreciated the fact that the counselor was trying to do his job. But obviously the counselor didn't understand; they were in love.

During that time with the counselor, Lindy had responded to the counselor by saying, "It's not like we don't know each other. We've been dating for a long time, and we hardly ever disagree about anything. In fact, we're probably compatible about everything."

She was saying that she had expectations resulting from previous experience with this relationship. It didn't do much good to tell Lindy that many people seem very compatible during the dating process. With the divorce rate as high as it is, this couple didn't want to hear that their dating relationship sounded like that of most couples.

Previous experience for most couples is the dating process. Their expectations are in for a shock! There's only one way to describe the whole dating situation. Dating is important. It gives people some basis for judgment about another person. But when it's all said and done, dating is a LIE.

One young woman, married for only a couple years, described dating as follows: "When we were dating, Bill did everything he could to be wonderful and win my hand. Bill is a salesman, and it seemed as if he viewed our relationship the same way he looked at his job. It was like he was after the biggest sale of his life. Then we got married, and it was like he finally made the sale. Once he made the sale, he didn't act like he had to do all those things anymore. He acted like he didn't have to service this account anymore."

The dating relationship is a very unrealistic relationship. Everyone puts his or her best foot forward. Both parties do everything they can to act in a way that will be appealing to the other person. No one with any brains would date a person and purposely show all his flaws. There is a significant amount of salesmanship involved in the dating process.

It's amazing how many people can date a person for several months, or even years, and then go into shock over the change in behavior their partner exhibits after the marriage. I think I heard my wife, Rosemary, say once that, "Bob and I dated for over five years and most of the time he was wonderful. Then almost immediately after the wedding he seemed to go brain dead. It was the same body but he sure was acting very differently."

As a man I had been trained to compete. I was willing and even motivated to compete for her hand in marriage. As to what came after that, I didn't have an inkling. I just figured I didn't need to compete anymore. I had already won the prize.

Those who get married and anticipate that married life will be just like the dating relationship are awakened from their honeymoon very quickly. Expectations built on dating experiences can be very unrealistic and very disappointing.

Previous Fantasies

All of us, men and women, carry our own special ideals about marriage. They're stored somewhere in the back of our hearts. They could have come from a special movie, a book, a favorite song, or just a story we have been told. They could even come from an unrealistic perception of a married couple we once knew. Once we have these ideals we often, consciously or subconsciously, create our own scenarios where we place ourselves in the picture.

During the period of dating, we often foster that fantasy relationship. We work hard at never letting the other person see us except when we look our best. We create a fantasy environment by acting as if we can always look perfect for the other person.

Persons who come from difficult home environments fantasize that this marriage will be a beautiful way of getting rescued. Many young woman who have been sexually abused have this rescue fantasy. Perhaps, after being abused at home, they see this young man as the knight who will rescue them from their troubles. But this is a fantasy. Women who count on a marriage to rescue them from the trauma of abuse carry their sexual difficulties right into their marriage bed.

Some young women who have been sexually abused at home enter into premarital sexual relationships with their fiancés. There may seem to be no sexual difficulties prior to the marriage, and then, almost the day after the wedding, major sexual problems enter the relationship. All of these problems need to be worked through with the help of a counselor. It is pure fantasy to believe that a wedding will solve the problems accompanying sexual abuse.

The fantasies we all carry, about the beauty of a wonderful marriage or wonderful sexual communication, can be a great hindrance to the first years of the marriage. Fantasies are often incorrect, and some are unobtainable. At the very least, they are unrealistic. The movies try to tell us we can meet, marry, and live in ecstasy the rest of our lives. If not, then we must not really be in love. But it's a fantasy. It's just the way they get us to watch the movie. It's a fantasy.

After a few years of marriage, when things don't go as planned, fantasies can lead us to believe two things. One is that no one can ever experience a fantastic marital relationship—those are just for dreamers. The other fantasy trap is that a real, wonderful, dreamy marriage was made possible by the "chemistry"—it just so happened that they were right for each other.

Both are very wrong. Marriages can be wonderful—they are meant to be wonderful. But they are wonderful as a result of concentrated effort. It takes work to make a great marriage, not chemistry.

Last summer we went with a close friend to his ranch in Jackson Hole, Wyoming. At our friend Gary's insistence, we spent one whole day climbing the side of a mountain to get to something he wanted us to see. We were both just exhausted, and it got to the point that we really didn't care what was in that special valley. It couldn't be worth all that pain we were going through. He just kept insisting. "Trust me," he kept saying, "you'll be glad you did this when we get there."

Three hours later, when our feet were blistered and we were dying of thirst, we finally reached our destination. Lying down on a side of a mountain, we were looking at the most beautiful valley and lake I had ever seen. The climb was long and it was agony, but it was more than worth it. Gary was right.

In the beginning, God established marriage. It wasn't meant to be easy; nothing worth having is. It was meant to be fulfilling and completing. It takes work, but it's almost as if God is saying, "Trust Me, it's worth the effort!"

Expectations can get in the way. Expectations can mislead a person. Marriage can be a wonderful relationship, but it does take work. More work than the dating relationship ever indicated.

Summary

1. Each person comes into the marriage with a basic set of expectations.

2. Previous observations of our parents' marriage or what we think our parents' marriage was like will impact the expectations we have about our own marriages.

3. Previous experiences in the relationship, such as dating, often prove to be invalid. Dating is a lie!

4. Previous fantasies, from novels, stories, or movies, can have a tremendous impact on our expectations about marriage.

Discussion Questions

1. What expectations did you bring into your marriage? What did you think your relationship was going to be like?

2. What expectations do you think your spouse brought into the marriage?

3. What is the source of your expectations? What do you think led you to anticipate the things you expected of the marriage (parents' marriage, relationship during dating, movies, etc.)? How realistic were these expectations?

4. How can you begin to resolve the differences between your expectations and reality?

3

Bilingual Marriage

Several years ago we had our first opportunity to present a marriage seminar to a group who did not speak English. One of us would speak a sentence and the person assigned to help us would then translate. When he finished translating our sentence, we would continue.

A very strange thing happened during this seminar. We would allow time for the translator to speak, and then wait for a laugh after a story that English-speaking people normally laughed at. But there was no laughter. It's difficult to say this and sound humble, but these are very funny stories which are usually received by uproarious laughter. Not this time, however.

Stranger yet, the audience began to laugh at times when we hadn't said anything funny. It was all very confusing for us, so when the first night of the conference was over we asked our translator to explain what was going on.

"I know English," he began to explain, "so I know that your talk was very funny. But it was only funny to English-speaking people. Your stories don't translate in a funny way. I knew that you were very humorous people, so I decided to make up some funny stories as I was translating. That's why the audience laughed at times when you didn't think you were funny."

The translator may have used the same words, but the jokes just didn't translate the same way. The marriage relationship has the same problem. Males and females just don't think the same way. As we relate to each other there seems to be a translation gap. The problem is that the people involved don't generally know that.

In the sixties and seventies, and even in the early eighties, we were all taught that the sexes were the same; we were supposed to be unisex. That philosophy didn't last long. In fact, it was an insult to both genders. Each gender comes into marriage with very special, individualized qualities. And we speak different "languages."

Each of us needs to understand what the other means; we need to be "bilingual" in our approach to life. Remember Lindy and John? He didn't have any problem making love after they had been arguing all evening. To Lindy, it was an insult to even suggest that they do something so intimate when they weren't getting along. Each person thought the other had a problem. But the problem was that they weren't allowing for the fact that each of them responded to life differently.

Bilingual Self-Esteem

The difference between men and women is apparent in the way we develop what we could call *adult self-esteem*. Quite often (but admittedly not always) the woman has learned to enhance her self-esteem by developing relationships, and she is able to maintain some very deep relationships. This is often evident in her relationship with her mother.

A man may say here, "Now wait a minute! I have a great relationship with my mom. I love my mom." That may be true, but how has he developed and maintained that relationship? How many times has he sat at lunch with his mom and talked for hours? How many hours has he spent on the phone this past month discussing things with his mom, or with anybody for that matter?

A woman usually has a stronger ability to relate to other persons and develop intimacy. It's one of the ways she feels good about herself. In fact, she often looks at marriage as the ultimate opportunity to develop intimacy.

A man, on the other hand, has not been taught to develop his self-esteem through relationships. Quite the contrary. In our culture men have been raised to compete with everyone around them. It's the "Little League syndrome" where men grow up doing everything they can to be able to beat Dad at Ping-Pong, foul shots, or anything. Men are raised to see those around them as objects of competition. It's difficult to have an intimate relationship with the people around you when you have been taught to keep up your guard. It's hard to communicate at a deep level when you can't or won't share your weaknesses.

Here's the difficulty (the bilingual-approach problem). A wife enters into marriage looking to share with her husband. She anticipates the opportunity to open up about problems and grow closer by becoming emotionally naked. She views the marriage as a way of enhancing the self-esteem of both of them.

Her husband, however, doesn't have any idea what she's talking about. He has been taught to raise his self-esteem through his work. The more he makes, the better he does, the higher he is promoted, the better his self-esteem.

The wife typically has a better handle on the workplace —it's a challenge to grow professionally, but it's not her life. He doesn't know any other way to feel good about himself.

She's looking to the marriage relationship to enhance her self-esteem, but she feels rejected, so she's suffering. He doesn't understand what a relationship is, so he's trying to find himself through work. He's hurting and lonely. He's dissatisfied and he doesn't know why.

They're both trying to work out their loneliness. The only difference is that she knows what the problem is—it's the fact that they aren't relating. He doesn't necessarily see the problem as a result of his not attempting to relate. In fact, he doesn't have any idea what to do.

Because the woman is more able to talk and is yearning for the relationship, the wife often suggests that they go for counseling. After all, talking about problems is something she knows how to do. He, on the other hand, doesn't know how to talk at that open or naked level, so he can't understand how a counselor could help. He's never opened up and shared at that level with anyone, let alone a stranger. He tends to think of counseling as a waste of time and money.

The Male Quest for Self-Esteem Outside Work

While men generally seek self-esteem from their work environment, men who are unhappy with their work still don't look to their marriages to meet their self-esteem needs. Indeed, they often look to other ways of competing to find fulfillment. Some men become so embroiled in softball leagues or other sports activities that, if they could, they would spend every waking hour out on the field. Rather than seeing sports as recreation, these men are looking for one more way to play "Little League."

Women Meeting Their Self-Esteem Needs Outside Marriage

When the marriage relationship is not meeting their self-esteem needs, as they had expected it would, women look elsewhere. It's only natural to do that as they search to have their self-esteem needs met. Some women dive totally into the lives of their children, their church, or civic activities. Other women have found themselves trapped in extramarital affairs, though they never meant to be unfaithful.

Other women have learned to find limited success going the male route. One man who came in for marital counseling found himself trying to combat this problem when it was too late. "I know that I created this problem," Tom stated to the counselor. "Years ago, when we both got out of graduate school, Donna begged me to not spend so much time at the office. Back then she saw her profession as a means to an end.

Unfortunately, I saw my profession as the end. I gave all my energies to my office and had nothing left for home. Donna eventually got tired of waiting for me to come home. Instead, she made a mental shift and decided to pour her life into her career. That was fine for me, and I even encouraged it. Then one day I woke up and realized that we didn't have a marriage. I asked her to back off her career as I would mine. But now she refuses. It's as if I hurt her for so many years that she doesn't want to risk being hurt ever again. I can't get her to work on our marriage anymore."

Donna waited for a long time to find happiness and fulfillment in her marriage relationship, then she just gave up and went the route that our culture teaches. Tom and Donna have many things that one would think should make a couple happy, but instead they are both miserable.

Bilingual Listening

Many couples attempt to communicate about their marital problems. She says, "I think we have to talk about our marriage." He says, "Okay, let's talk." When they finally sit down to talk, one of two things usually takes place. In the first scenario, she talks about how he has hurt her feelings and doesn't spend any time with her. He says, "Oh, that's ridiculous. We watched television together all evening." He tells her it's ridiculous, because he doesn't yet know how to talk at a feeling level. He can answer the objective question about time spent together, but subjective things like feelings don't compute.

In the second scenario, she just wants to spend time talking. The conversation may be about what she perceives as their problem. As soon as she says what the problem is, he thinks she wants him to fix it. He immediately wants to stop the conversation and offer a solution. There! Done! End of conversation. Now they can get on to more productive things.

She doesn't necessarily want him to offer an instant solution; she just wants him to talk and listen. She just wants to relate. He just wants to find a way to conquer the difficulty. That's the way their self-esteems are. For her it's to relate. For him it's to fix or conquer. And they both become very frustrated.

"I don't want you to listen for three minutes and then fix it," Rosemary has said to me many times. "I just want to spend time talking about it."

That's the most difficult thing for the male to compute. "What do you mean you don't want me to offer a solution? Why are we even talking about this if you don't want to look for answers?" Why? Because we're different in the way we communicate.

In the Bible, when God created the institution of marriage it was for a specific reason. He looked at Adam and realized that it wasn't good for him to be alone. In other words, he wasn't going to make it by himself. He had skills in some areas, but he was definitely lopsided. So God created the rest of the plan. God sent Eve to complete the assignment. It was her job to teach him how to relate.

Grow Because of Your Bilingualism

It's our job to see each other's strengths and needs. Generally, her strengths are in the area of relationship. He can ignore her strengths and the relationship and continue feeling unfulfilled himself. Or he can decide to learn from her skills of relating.

When she indicates a desire to develop the relationship, he should take advantage of the opportunity to learn from it.

Just Because I Don't Understand It Doesn't Mean It's Not Valid

In 1973, one year after our wedding, Rosemary and I decided to spend part of the summer in Europe. It was far from a luxury trip, as we traveled on the European Rail system and stayed in hostels. One of Rosemary's dreams was to see the great art museums of Europe. One museum was enough for me. I realized very quickly that these museums didn't have any food and I was bored.

It was surprising to me how much time she could spend standing in front of those paintings. They didn't mean anything to me. The difference was that she had spent part of her life being taught about the great artists of the world. She had the background, so she was able to take it all in and enjoy it.

Toward the end of our stay in Europe I, too, began to be able to enjoy these museums because I let her teach me about what we were looking at. Until then, we were looking at the same works of art but seeing very different things. I was seeing pictures by guys who couldn't paint straight lines. She was seeing the greatest works of art the world had to offer. Yet we were both looking at the same thing. It took working together to enjoy that. Otherwise, I would only have been waiting impatiently to leave so I could find something to eat!

There's no doubt about it. Individuals enter into the marriage speaking different languages. They experience things differently. They talk and listen differently. And they love and grow their self-esteem differently. Marriage can be tough unless the couple is willing to set aside some time to learn from each other.

It must be said that the way the two genders are described here is a generalization. In some marriages the roles are reversed—he is much more able to describe his feelings, and she is the one who is not skilled in this area. Whichever way it is in your marriage, the key is to understand it, accept it, and go from there. When you think about it, it's a perfect plan. With both of us being different, we can experience life to the maximum. All because we each relate to life from different perspectives.

Summary

1. Marriage partners often look at the same marriage in very different ways. She sees it as an opportunity to enhance

her self-esteem by developing the relationship. He sees it as one more thing on his list of things he's done, but looks to his place of work to develop his self-esteem.

2. Each person must understand that his or her partner experiences the relationship differently.

3. Couples must be willing to sit down and spend time talking about these differences.

4. It's important to acknowledge that these differences are an asset.

Discussion Questions

1. What does your spouse do that makes you feel loved and respected?

2. What does your spouse do that makes you feel he or she doesn't understand your needs? What does your spouse do that makes you feel lonely?

3. What does your spouse do that makes you feel like it's okay to share your feelings? What does he or she do to open the door to talking?

4. What are the things that you feel shut down the communication?

5. What can each of you do to take advantage of your differences?

Part 2

Choose to Be Married

4

Opposites Attract

My grandfather had a fabulous farm in Colorado. He used to tell me about the difference between those who had a farm and those who were farmers. "There are many people who own farms," Grandfather would say. "Some got them from their parents, some ended up farming while looking for something to do, and some bought a farm trying to get back to nature. Then there are those of us who are farmers because we choose to be farmers. Every day we get up and make that choice. Much of the time it's not fun, but we still choose to do farming instead of anything else. I can walk on people's farms and tell you which kind they are. Whether they choose to farm or just have a farm."

I remember asking Grandfather what he was going to do with the farm after he retired. "There's no retiring from something you love, Bobby. But when I hit the point where I can no longer properly farm, I'll sell it." I couldn't believe my ears. "How could you sell it when you love it so much?" I asked incredulously. "Why don't you leave it to one of the kids so you can keep it going?"

His answer to that question has always stuck with me. "None of the children has chosen to farm. No one has come to spend a summer farming. Several of you have shown a passing interest and asked about farming, but none of you has actually chosen to farm. It's a decision you have to make rather than something you casually do."

Grandfather's philosophy on farming translates to anything worth doing in life, but there are few things that it fits

43

better than the marriage relationship. We must choose to be married.

Many people get married. That's an action we take on a given day, but it doesn't have much to do with the rest of our lives unless we make a conscious choice. There seem to be many who get married and then go on with life as if nothing has happened except for the fact that they are living with another person. They don't really change the way they look at things or the way they make decisions. They don't choose to be married.

When Did We Get So Different?

There are few things about a marriage that need a conscious choice more than the fact that spouses seem to be so different. The very fact that opposites attract brings an element to the marriage relationship that causes choice. Choose to deal with the differences or choose to let them irritate.

It's amazing how similar our interests seem to be when we are dating. And while the ways we approach things are different, when we're dating, we don't seem to notice or care.

For some reason I'm neat to the point of being obnoxious to everyone around me. When Rosemary and I were dating, I thought it was cute that she didn't find it important to take care of details. I'll never forget the first time I looked inside the desk in her apartment. Each drawer looked like a grenade had gone off in it. I thought it was funny and straightened it up for her. The fact that we were so different in several areas never bothered me at all—when we were dating.

Then we got married. One day, after we returned from our honeymoon, we were folding the laundry together. She opened the underwear drawer of my dresser, and I heard her burst out laughing. I walked over to see what was so hilarious, but nothing seemed to be out of order. In fact, that was it.

"What's so funny?" I asked. She just stood there pointing and then said, "This is ridiculous. All your shorts are rolled up in these neat little packets, row after row. I can't believe it."

"What's so funny about that?" I asked. "You want to see something funny, take a look at that disaster where you put your underwear. Everything is jammed in so tightly that nothing else will fit. If a burglar broke into our apartment and opened your underwear drawer, all your lingerie would explode out all over him. It would take weeks to find him!"

Then Rosemary said sarcastically, "How could you stand living with such a slob?"

To which I arrogantly replied, "You'll see the error of your ways."

That was funny that particular day, but our differences began to be a source of irritation. Everything she did seemed to be done the wrong way. When we'd talk about it, she would tell me that I spent an incredible amount of time worrying about things that don't really matter. *But they do matter*, I thought. *The way the forks go in the dishwasher does matter if you want to make the most of the space.*

It all culminated on a day during our first year of marriage when I made a very profound mistake. I was waiting on the couch for Rosemary to finish getting ready to go out to eat and decided that I wanted a piece of gum. Her purse was right there, so I opened it in search of gum. I know, that was my first mistake.

When I opened her purse I was in shock at the things I found. Receipts from things she had purchased back in the 1800s, old gum wrappers, etc. So I decided to help her out. Yes, I decided to clean her purse. It just shows how ignorant or arrogant I was back then.

Rosemary came out of the bedroom and saw me cleaning her purse and went into shock! To make matters worse, I was smiling. I thought I was being helpful. That night we had a very interesting time at dinner. Now that I think about it, I'm surprised she even went with me to dinner.

"You really think that your way of doing things, in fact, your way of living in general, is the right way and my way is the wrong way, don't you?" She began with that opener, but never let me answer because she was so mad. "No, it's more than that. You think that you're God's gift to me, to help straighten out and organize my life. I was doing fine before you started straightening me out and, as I recall, you used to think it was nice that I was different. Now it seems to me something has happened. Now you seem to get irritated when I don't put the forks away in perfect rows. For some reason you have chosen to change your mind about the way I am. Now you seem to think that I need to be changed. Why is that?"

Wow! That was quite a mouthful. We didn't solve the problem that night at dinner. But what we did decide to do was talk about it. She was right. I had chosen to accept her the way she was when we were dating, but then, after the wedding, for some reason I changed my mind. It wasn't anything I did consciously, but I had *chosen* to get upset about the way she did some of the things she did.

Choose to Accept

It's all in the basic choices we must make. One key choice is to decide to love and accept our spouses for who they are, rather than who we think we're supposed to make them. It sounds so basic, but if we don't think the decision through, we'll miss doing it—and we'll go right on judging where they leave their shoes, how they squeeze the tube, the way they park the car. We'll see all these things as mistakes. It's very narrow-minded of any person to think that there is only one right way to do things.

Of course, sometimes I think I can even explain why my way is the only way. That's the epitome of arrogance. Actually, it's immaturity.

My way isn't the right way, it's just one way. We each must choose to accept our spouses for who they are without arrogantly trying to make them like us. If we don't consciously make that choice, then it won't be long until everything our spouses do gets very irritating. The way she loads the dishwasher, the way she keeps old receipts in her purse—in fact, the way she does anything that is the least bit different from the way I do it. I must choose to accept that difference.

Choose to Blend

A couple here in town is in medical practice together. It's amazing how different they are. She's very outgoing and friendly, and he's very quiet and methodical. They seemed to be the most unlikely people to be married. Yet not only are they married, but they have a successful practice that seems to have sprung up overnight.

I remember asking how they were able to do so well together when they seem so different. "Oh, the fact that I'm loud and Jack is quiet is only one of an incredible number of differences," Linda began. "We are different in the way we do almost everything, and it drove us crazy. Jack is real good when it comes to dealing with the accounting part of a practice, and I don't even balance a checkbook. But I'm good at dealing with all the salesmen who walk into this clinic. Jack, on the other hand, would end up buying everything they showed him.

"When we first got out of school we were advised not to go into practice together, so we didn't. For several years we each practiced with somebody else. We did it for the sake of our marriage. A funny thing was happening, however. I'd bring my billing books home to ask Jack to look at them, and he'd ask me to call a certain drug salesman back for him and cancel his order.

"We weren't in practice with each other, but we were relying on each other's strengths. One day it occurred to us that we could do well together, so we left where we were and opened a practice together."

The story of this couple's new practice doesn't end happily ever after at this point, however. When they went into practice together, it went well for about a month and then they started to make each other crazy. They couldn't get along at the office, and they brought those problems home. She didn't keep the rooms at the office as professionally as he thought they should be, and he didn't answer all the patients' questions the way she thought he should. His patients were coming to her with their questions. All they did was argue.

Jack made an interesting statement when he looked back at those times. "It's amazing how I allowed my strengths to accentuate her weaknesses and vice versa. And she was choosing for her strengths to make me look inept. Our strengths should have complemented each other's weaknesses beautifully, but they weren't. They weren't because we weren't letting them."

It was at that point that this couple went for counseling. Through counseling and talking they were able to make a life-changing choice. They would not only choose to accept their differences, but they would also go the next step. If one person had an ability in one area and it was an ability that they both acknowledged, the team would use it.

Working as a Team

A wide receiver can run and catch the ball. He's gifted in that area. When it's a play that calls for blocking, however, they usually call in another player. They try not to put the receiver in a position to do something he's not good at.

In our marriages, once we've worked through the fact that we are different, the next step is to accept that fact. We need to accept the differences and not try to make our spouses like us. Once we can do this, we're ready to grow as a team. First we need to recognize that our spouses have gifts in certain areas. But that's not enough. We need to be mature enough to say, "This is something you do better than I do. How do you think we should do it?"

I tend to be a very rigid father, as if you couldn't have guessed. It can be hard on our children and get in the way of our parent/child relationship when I get overly structured about things. Rosemary, on the other hand, is much more relationship-oriented. Many times I have to sit and ask her, "Am I getting ridiculous about this issue?" It kills me to hear her say, "Yes." It's at those times I have to choose to step out of my rigid comfort zone and choose to lean on her area of strength—her gift of seeing what really needs to be done.

If you don't choose to accept each other the way you are, you lose. If you don't choose to lean on each other's strengths rather than fight, you lose. Let's face it, if you don't choose you lose.

Summary

1. Getting married is an event that takes only one day. Being married is something we must choose to do every day.

2. Accepting the different ways your spouse does things is a conscious choice you must make.

3. Choose to utilize each other's strengths and become a better team.

4. Only in a step of maturity can you choose to allow your partner to use his or her strengths when they accentuate your area of weakness.

Discussion Questions

1. It never ceases to amaze me how I can get bothered about the way the knives, forks, and spoons are placed in the dishwasher. It's amazing how worked up I can get about these little differences in the way we each think things should be done. Describe the areas of your life where you and your spouse see things differently. In other words, what are those little things that you argue about?

2. Sometimes we forget our spouse's strengths. Many times our spouses don't think we believe they have any strengths. Make a list of the personality strengths your spouse has. Are there areas where your spouse's strengths could be better utilized?

3. For many couples it boils down to using the best of each other's gifts. For our marriage it was deciding to sit down and

talk honestly about our different approaches to life and then developing a plan to work as a team.

Develop a plan that allows you to function better as a team. Emphasize each other's strengths. What night are you going to sit down and talk about it?

Further Reading on This Topic

Marriage Personalities, David Field, Harvest House.

5

Choosing to Be Friends

Spouses must choose to be friends. Now doesn't that sound ridiculous? Of course we're friends. We're married. We do things together. Let's face it, we must be friends.

Let's take a minute to look at how friends treat each other. Let's say it's eleven o'clock Friday night, and I'm getting ready for bed. The phone rings; it's my friend Mike. "Bob, I hate to call you at this hour, but I'm out on Highway 27 and I've run out of gas. I'm calling you from my car phone because there aren't any gas stations around."

Before Mike could go any further with the conversation, I would cut in. Not wanting to make him feel bad about the hour of his call I might say something like, "Mike, no problem. I was just finishing doing one hundred push-ups. Where are you on Highway 27? Tell me what exit you're near. I'll get my gas can from the garage and stop by the all-night gas station. I should be there in about twenty minutes. Just sit tight."

When I finally arrive with the gas he would probably say something like, "I can't tell you how grateful I am for this help." I respond, "Hey, thanks for calling me. After all, what are friends for?" Isn't that gracious? I'm actually thanking him for getting me out of bed in the middle of the night.

Friendship is quite a special relationship. We don't mind being inconvenienced for a friend. As a matter of fact, subconsciously, we look for ways to add more building blocks to our friendship, taking advantage of opportunities to be helpful or comforting.

Now picture this next, very real scene. It's five o'clock in the afternoon, and Rosemary calls me just before I leave my office for home. "Bob, are you on your way home?" To which I would respond in the affirmative. "Would you do me a favor? Would you stop by the store on your way home and get us a gallon of milk?"

After a moment of silence, in a very irritated tone, I would respond with, "Rosemary! You've got to be kidding. That would mean pulling all the way across Sheridan Street in this heavy traffic, through the drive-through, and then out again. That means an extra five minutes, plus risking my life crossing Sheridan Street again. What were you doing today that you couldn't remember to get milk?"

Mike's request took over an hour out of the middle of my night. My wife's request could be done while I was already going in that direction, past the store, to get some milk for my kids. But I didn't quite respond in the same gracious way.

What's the difference in these two responses? In one response I'm trying to be a friend. In the second response not only am I not trying to be a friend, but I'm trying to avoid even being helpful. I'm taking the relationship for granted.

Being a Friend Is Something You Decide to Decide

Remember the last time someone new moved onto your street? Whether you actually did this or not, you meant to. When you saw the moving van and then the family pull up, you decided you would make them a cake or something neighborly like that. You thought about going out of your way to be a good neighbor. Perhaps you even invited them over to eat. You made a decision to be a friend even though you didn't know them.

Isn't it amazing that we'll choose to act in a friendly way toward people that don't mean anywhere near as much to us as our spouses do. But when it actually comes to our spouses, we act like it's too much effort. It's all in the attitude we choose. It's a decisive attitude with the people outside our families, but it's a lazy attitude with our family members. That's often especially true when it comes to our spouses.

Lazy attitudes toward our spouses often come because we let ourselves take the other person for granted. We've been married for so long that we subconsciously feel as if we don't have to be nice or helpful or even friendly.

Larry and Lannie were in a counselor's office for help with their marriage. They were discussing this very thing, the fact that they treat other people better than they treat each other. "A perfect example of what we're talking about happened the other night," Lannie began with tears welling up in her eyes. "I couldn't believe what I saw. When we finished dinner at Elaine's house, you got up from the table, helped clear all the dishes, and then offered to rinse everything. Elaine said to me later, 'Larry certainly is a wonderful husband. I hope you know how fortunate you are.'"

Lannie went on to say that it hurt her deeply that Larry would act like the perfect, concerned, helpful husband when others were watching, but that he hadn't touched a dish or helped clear the table in their own house for over ten years. When Larry responded defensively that he would try to be more helpful at home, Lannie responded with, "That's not the point. I'm not talking about getting you to be more helpful at home. I'm saying that it hurt me to see you go out of your way to help someone else, but you wouldn't do those things for me. You were considerate of Elaine's needs and not of mine."

It's common. We're on our best behavior when we're out in public. It's natural for us to want people to think of us as nice. My whole neighborhood probably thinks that I'm the most wonderful person in the world. When I take out the garbage I'm friendly. I even offered to help one of the neighbors who had a dozen bags of lawn clippings and leaves. *Bob is really a great guy*, my neighbor must have thought. *His family sure is lucky.* I won't go into what happens to my friendly attitude when I walk back into my house. Suffice it to say that when I return to my family, behind closed doors, many times the radiant smile falls off and I stop campaigning for public office.

Unfriendliness Can Become a Habit

Once we do something enough times it can become a habit. We don't even know we are doing something in a particular way or with a specific attitude. That was the most difficult part of the problem between Larry and Lannie. He really didn't realize what he was doing. Larry wanted to work on his marriage, but when Lannie talked to him about different aspects of their relationship, he just thought she was being overly sensitive.

"How else do I treat you less than human?" Larry asked sarcastically. All this was painful for him to hear because it came as a surprise. "You don't treat me sub-human, Larry, you just don't seem to treat me like a friend anymore. When we were dating, we'd go out to eat and you would listen to everything I had to say. You'd look me right in the eye and actually listen. Now you listen to everybody but me."

"Oh, that's ridiculous!" Larry cut in. "You're just overreacting again."

"Can I finish what I wanted to say?" Lannie asked. "Last weekend, when we were eating with Jack and Elaine, you had a totally different attitude toward them when they were talking than you did when I was talking. When either of them was saying something you looked them right in the eye and listened. I watched and saw you looking as if you really wanted to understand what they were saying. When I began to talk I was the only adult at the table that you didn't bother to look at. In fact, you acted as if you were just waiting for me to finish talking so you could get on with the conversation. I felt tolerated rather than loved.

"Larry, I never even thought about this until a couple of weeks ago when Debbie (their seven-year-old daughter) asked me why you listen to all her friends' stories and not hers. When I asked her why she thought that, she said, "When my friends spent the night Daddy sat with us for a while, and when my friends told their stories Daddy looked at them and listened, but when I told mine, Daddy just got up and walked around." When she said that I realized that was exactly what was happening with me, too."

Larry had developed a habit of showing concern for other people and their feelings, but he wasn't working on the relationships in his home anymore. It's not that he didn't love his family. He loved them all very much. It was that he had gotten a little rusty in the area of trying to be a full-time friend to the people he loved the most.

It's the Little Things That Count

Being a friend requires decisive action. It necessitates asking oneself questions like, "How can I help this person that I love?" Of course, this applies not just to the big things in life, but also to the little day-to-day things such as dishes, or whatever those little special gestures happen to be.

So often many of us feel that we plug away through life doing the hard things, making a living, taking care of the kids, painting the house, ironing the clothes, things that are the long-haul gestures. If we do those things, many of us believe we're doing enough. But those are obligatory. Rather than gestures, they are responsibilities. Friends do things that go beyond obligation.

Gestures of Friendship

Gestures of friendship are different for each person. Gestures of friendship are those little special things that one person does for another person. Gestures are not necessarily big things. That's one of the problems with our culture today. We start to believe the marketing promotions that say a real gesture of

friendship is buying her a diamond bracelet. The advertise-
ments make us believe that that's a real gesture. Unfortunately,
we can't all afford to buy diamond bracelets. And even if we
could, such gestures would be very far apart from each other.
You can't buy a diamond every week.

At its best, a gesture of friendship is something that
doesn't cost much but has a significant ingredient. It's out of
the giver's comfort zone or thinking range. In other words, it's
a gesture that the giver would not automatically do or necessarily want in return.

After several counseling sessions Larry and Lannie came
into the office, and Lannie made an announcement. "This has
been the best week we've had in years!" Thinking that they had
received an inheritance or found the cure for cancer, I asked
what had happened. "Larry bought me two cards this week that
were very affectionate, and he mailed them from his office."

Larry was obviously proud of himself, but he also looked a
little perplexed. When I asked him how he felt about Lannie's
reaction to his cards he said, "To tell you the truth, I was
shocked at how much they meant to her. After all, these were
two cards written by some poet and printed in the thousands.
Yet she loved them. I'm sure glad I picked out the right ones!"

"It's not the words in the cards, silly," Lannie interrupted,
grabbing his hand affectionately. "It's the fact that you went
out of your way to get them for me. It's the fact that I know
that cards don't mean much to you, but you got them for me
because they mean a lot to me. It's what they represent . . .
(then she said it) . . . that you're trying to be my friend."

Larry had listened to her needs and tried to meet those
needs, whether or not he understood them. That was a gesture of friendship. Exhibiting gestures of friendship is one at-
tribute of being a friend. Larry and Lannie were beginning to
renew their friendship after several years of marriage. It was
the start of two people deciding to not only be married but
also to be friends. In the next chapter we address other attributes of friendship.

Summary

1. Being a friend to your spouse is something you must decide to do.

2. Being a friend is often difficult because friendship requires gestures. Sometimes these gestures mean quite a lot to one spouse, yet they wouldn't mean anything to the other spouse.

3. Being a friend to your spouse means coming out of your comfort zone.

4. Deciding to be a friend to your spouse means breaking old habits of "lazy attitudes" that come from taking your spouse and your relationship for granted.

Discussion Questions

1. Ask your spouse this question: "What can I do to be a better friend to you? Tell me some little gesture that would be meaningful to you."

2. How can you step out of your comfort zone by doing something for your spouse that he or she enjoys but that you don't particularly like doing? What, specifically, could you do?

3. What is the biggest area of friendship that you think is missing in your marriage? (Some possibilities include a friend/spouse that listens when you talk, a friend/spouse who chooses to be helpful, a friend/spouse who unselfishly does the hard or dirty jobs.) What can be done to change that area?

4. Think of a best friend from the past. What about that relationship made him or her a best friend? Is that ingredient in your marriage?

5. What is one area of friendship you plan to change in your marriage?

6

Attributes of a Friend

In the previous chapter Lannie told her husband, Larry, about a time when they were at a friend's house and he had acted like a perfect husband. In fact, that's what Lannie's friend said to her. "Lannie, Larry certainly is a wonderful husband. I hope you know how fortunate you are." After the counseling session, Larry was more than a little curious to know what Lannie had said to their friend Elaine when she praised Larry for being the perfect husband.

"How did you answer Elaine when she said that about me?" Larry asked.

"I felt like telling her what I really thought," Elaine answered. "I felt like saying, 'This is a nice show, but he never does it when he's home.' But I didn't. I just said, 'Larry's a great guy.'"

"Why?" Larry wanted to know. "Why didn't you tell her what you really thought?"

Lannie responded with a very significant answer. "I wasn't going to be disloyal to you. Why would I say something bad about you?"

All Larry could say to that was, "Thanks."

Friends Are Loyal

Lannie thought her friend's assessment of Larry's helpfulness was ridiculous, but she wasn't going to betray her husband. Friends are like that. Friends don't criticize their friends to other people. They certainly confront issues of disagreement to their friend's faces, but they aren't disloyal outside the relationship.

Many couples are married for so long that they use their spouses to get laughs. They tell jokes about their spouses that are critical or demeaning. Other people actually compete with their spouses without realizing it.

Some time ago we were at a dinner party and found ourselves sitting at a table with a couple we didn't know. The man at the party was obviously a little nervous about this situation, so we began to pull him out by asking questions about his work. The man began telling a story about a recent event in his career, but every time he gave a detail his wife corrected it. "It wasn't a Friday when that happened, it was a Thursday," she cut in. "It wasn't Cincinnati, it was Cleveland." It went on and on until he just gave up. It wasn't important to him to tell the story anymore. Yet it was still important for her to show everyone that she was a detail person and that she knew just how everything happened. So she finished his story.

At the end of the night the woman came up to us and thanked us for sitting at their table. She closed with, "He doesn't really like coming to these dinners very much." We wanted to say to her that we didn't blame him. We didn't like sitting at the table with her either.

Loyalty in marriage means that you let the small things go by. Loyalty means that you don't correct your teammate in public. When your spouse is getting all the attention being loyal means that you stand back and cheer rather than interrupt or get jealous.

Some spouses find it difficult to let their partners tell an interesting story or joke when they are together in public. Rather than sitting back and enjoying the fact that their spouse is getting the attention, they have to interrupt. Thinking that she's not telling it fast enough or that he's emphasizing the wrong details, the spouse cuts in. Worse than that is when one spouse is telling a funny story and the other spouse jumps in and tells the punch line. He just couldn't let the spouse get all the attention.

We wouldn't be that rude to a friend or co-worker at the office. If we did, they would probably say something to us. Yet when it comes to our marriage partners we often just go right ahead and walk all over their stories or jokes. We act as if they have no feelings. Marital friends support each other when they are in public; they don't compete.

Friends Do the Nasty Jobs—Without Being Asked

"I am sick and tired of having to tell you when I need help around the house," Diane blurted out, fighting back the tears.

"If you don't tell me, how am I supposed to know?" Mike responded in bewilderment.

"I don't believe that, Mike. I don't believe that you don't notice when I need help. I think that you just ignore me." Mike looked back at his wife as if she had just made a ridiculous accusation.

This time, however, Diane was prepared with an illustration. "All right!" Diane began, all but screaming at him. "All right, I'll prove to you that you ignore me when I need help!"

Diane began by asking Mike if he remembered last weekend when they were planning to go for a bike ride. "I remember only that when it was finally time to go, you didn't want to go anymore," Mike responded.

They had planned to pack a snack and ride their bikes over to a local park. Mike was ready to go, but Diane had to finish some of the household chores. The dishwasher wasn't working, so she had to wash breakfast dishes, as well as all the dishes from the night before. They had entertained company that previous night, so it was a huge pile.

Before beginning the dishes, Diane went out into the laundry room to sort the laundry and put in the first load of wash. It was going to take quite a while until she was ready to go to the park. As she walked into the laundry room she noticed Mike picking up the newspaper and sitting in his favorite chair.

The fact that he didn't see her need for help grated on her nerves, but she tried to justify his insensitivity. After all, he had gotten up earlier than she did and had gotten his own chores done. As she walked into the laundry room she said over her shoulder, "It's going to be quite a while 'til I'm ready to go. I've still got all of last night's dishes to do." *Maybe he'll take the hint,* she thought. She could just be blunt and ask him to help her, but she knew that he'd only say, "I offered to help last night before we went to bed, and you said that you'd take care of it this morning." *Surely he'll notice that I need help.*

Ten minutes later she walked back into the kitchen, looking first at the sink to see if he had noticed the need for help. It didn't really surprise her that he wasn't standing at the sink washing dishes. He hadn't noticed her need. What did surprise her, however, was the fact that he did notice someone else's need.

Mike wasn't reading the paper anymore. Diane could see him in the new neighbor's backyard helping the man put up a swing set. This neighbor had just moved in behind them, and obviously Mike had looked out the window and had seen the man working. Seeing a neighbor's need, he rushed to assist. That was all Diane could take. She started the dishes and then left them half done and got in the car to go for a ride and a cry.

"Where did you go?" Mike asked when she returned an hour later. Before she could even answer, Mike said, "Come look out the window." Mike took her to the window and proudly pointed to the swing set that he had helped build. Ironically, they were looking out the window that was over the sink of yet-unfinished dishes. Diane just walked away.

Now, a few days later, they were talking about the incident. Diane said "All you remember about last weekend was that I didn't want to go for a bike ride. Do you want to know why?" Mike responded with, "Of course I want to know why. That's why I asked you about fifty times."

"I needed help last Saturday," Diane began to explain. "We had all the dishes to do and the laundry. I couldn't go for a bike ride until I got those things done. I could have asked you for help. In fact, I kind of did when I told you about how much I had to do. But I didn't want to bug you since you had already gotten up early to get all your chores done. I figured you were just tired and done with working for the day. When I came back in from the laundry room, I saw that you didn't want to help me, but that you went out of your way to make yourself available for a stranger . . . that just did me in."

A friend senses a need and takes on the difficult jobs. It's one thing to respond pleasantly when asked for help, but it's an even greater friend who sees a need and goes after the job without being asked for help. That's what being a friend is all about. Even a casual acquaintance will offer assistance when asked.

Friends, on the other hand, will go out of their way to find out if they can help. They don't wait to be asked.

As marriage partners, we must learn to adopt an attitude that allows us to detect when our spouses need help. Put a better way, we must focus on being a friend to our partners. I drive home from work each day right into the western sun. The sun is intense enough for me to need to put down the visor on my car. The underside of that visor has a picture of each of my family members clipped to it. As I flip down the visor, there they are, looking me right in the eye as if to say to me, "We're the ones you're coming home for. Please don't ignore us when you get there."

Friends don't wait to be asked. Friends roll up their sleeves and take on the tough jobs. That's because friends can't relax until their best friend can relax with them.

A Friend Overlooks the Minor Cracks

It's amazing how we tend to forgive our friends for their flaws. We have a friend who is hilarious to be around and who would do anything if you needed help. He is often very obnoxious, however. This individual is extremely pigheaded about many issues and will not allow for any compromise. He's so argumentative that he will know this paragraph is referring to him and he'll say to himself, *Yeah, that's me all right!* It's sometimes exhausting for us to be with him because our opinions on so many things are so different, and many times we end up arguing.

When asked by someone else, "How can you stand being around that guy?" I have a very natural response: "Who, Fred? He's my friend."

That response comes naturally because Fred has so many other redeeming qualities. I choose to overlook the fact that he lacks tact. It's a natural response to have toward a friend.

Why is it, then, that I seem to pick at every single difference in my marriage partner? We don't have to disagree on the big things for me to get irritated. She can just put the toothpaste back in the wrong place and I'm irritated, not to mention that she squeezes it incorrectly.

I know ahead of time that she's going to be a few minutes late as we leave for church. Yet I still sit in the car, irritated, with the engine running. I choose to accept my friend the way he is. Why is it that I already know the way my spouse is and how she's going to respond to things, yet I allow myself to get mad at her for these differences?

Perhaps I don't really allow myself to get irritated. Maybe I choose to get irritated. Maybe we know that we exhibit many flaws of our own and so, consciously or subconsciously, we like to make sure the scale is balanced. If I acknowledge the fact that my spouse has flaws, too, it makes us feel less inadequate.

In other words, I know that I have immaturities and I don't always carry my end of the marriage bargain. After all, we live together, so I know she knows all about my flaws. And my flaws are so much more apparent to my spouse than to anybody else. Knowing I have flaws that stick out loud and clear, I can either work on improving myself or I can point out my spouse's flaws. Pointing out the flaws in my spouse is like saying, "See, you're not perfect either!" I already know she's going to be late getting in the car to leave for church. I just want to make sure she knows I know. That way she can't belabor the fact that I forgot to take the garbage out again yesterday. Now that I think about it, maybe I'll honk the horn so the neighbors will also know she's late!

That's a pretty mature way for an adult to act, isn't it! I know that you realize I'm only kidding. Who would actually act in such a childish way? Certainly not us—after all, we're writing this book. Ha!

When we make the choice to befriend our spouses, we must choose to ignore the insignificant blemishes. In many cases our differences were some of the things that attracted us to our spouses when we were dating. It's not fair to hold those things against them now. A friend is someone who chooses not to make a big deal over the things that don't really matter. Don't major on the minors. Disconnect your horn.

A Friend Protects the Nakedness

"You want me to share with you, but then you beat me with it." Joe and Joanie were sitting in the counselor's office, telling each other how this "sharing stuff doesn't work." What Joe was really saying was that sharing from the heart was too risky. It gave his spouse a weapon. He had risked a conversation where he revealed some deep feelings or emotions. He had risked emotional nakedness.

They had taken the counselor's advice and gone on their weekly date night. Part of the homework they were given was to learn to share or talk about things that were difficult for them to discuss. For Joe, most things, especially weaknesses, were difficult for him to reveal.

Joanie had been concerned that Joe was not the spiritual leader in the home. Joe was aware of that difficulty between them, and they were talking about why he was timid when it came to teaching the children. "Joanie, I didn't grow up in a

Christian home like you did," Joe explained during their date. "I know this is no justification, but I don't have any idea how to lead the children in family devotions."

They discussed this further, and Joanie was delighted to hear her husband's openness. She'd never heard him say he didn't know how to do anything, let alone ask her for help. They decided that Joanie would buy a children's devotional and Joe would start reading it to the children at breakfast.

The process began and, as awkward as Joe sounded leading the prayer time, Joanie was delighted. Joe felt inadequate and a little foolish trying to do something he didn't know how to do, but it was worth the risk.

Then the explosion went off. Saturday morning Joanie and Joe were standing behind the soccer bench of their oldest son's game. Their son didn't see them there and the boy was overheard using a couple of four-letter words. Joanie and Joe were shocked. Then Joanie, in her total desperation, turned to Joe and said, "See, if you had been the spiritual leader you needed to be this kind of thing would never have happened!"

Joe was shocked. "Joanie, that's not true and it's not fair," he responded. Joanie shot back without thinking, "What do you mean it's not true. You even admitted the other night that you weren't the spiritual leader you needed to be. Now look what's happened."

A week later they were in the counselor's office. Joanie wanted to talk and open up. Not Joe. He had done that, and look what happened. When the going got rough, Joanie used his openness to beat him. She didn't protect his nakedness. When he got emotionally naked and revealed weakness, she didn't treat it as sacred. Instead, she mistakenly used it as ammunition.

Many years ago there was a great football quarterback who hurt his knee and needed surgery. It was back when knee surgery meant that your knee was cut all the way open and the surgeon went inside. When the quarterback finally was able to come back to football, he came out on the field with a huge bandage wrapped around that knee. It must have looked like a target for the opposing defense to shoot for because he didn't last very long. They went after his weakness and ended his career.

Many times when marriage partners reveal or admit to weaknesses, their spouses are blessed by such openness. Other times, however, spouses use those times of sharing as a weapon. When they need ammunition to win an argument they go to their bag of dirty tricks. The saddest comment I ever heard was, "If you weren't having these sexual problems we wouldn't be having this discussion!"

Friends protect each other's back. They hold sacred the weaknesses of their spouses. Friends never use the weakness of a spouse to prove a point or win an argument. Marriage partners must vow not to play dirty but instead to protect the heart of the one they love.

Summary

1. Friends are loyal. They don't feel compelled to make fun of their spouses in public. They don't feel the need to correct the details of a story their spouses are telling. They're not rude, they're loyal.

2. Friends look for ways to help their spouses. Even when they aren't asked. Even when it means taking on the nasty jobs.

3. Friends ignore their spouses' flaws.

4. Friends guard their spouses' nakedness. Friends never use weaknesses against each other. They hold as sacred those things a spouse might reveal in a time of emotional truthfulness.

Discussion Questions

1. What area of need can you meet in the daily routine of your partner's life?

2. What is it that your spouse doesn't do when you need help? Why does it irritate you so much?

3. Is it worth the irritation that you go through? How could you explain it to your spouse in a way that he or she could understand?

4. Are there things that you do or say that are disloyal to the marriage friendship? How can you correct this situation?

5. Friends overlook the minor flaws in each other's lives. What flaw would you like your spouse to stop badgering you about? Is it something that can easily be overlooked?

6. Is it safe to share a weaknesses with your spouse? Does he or she use it against you? Are you a safe person to share with? Give examples so that you and your spouse can better understand areas where you both feel the other has been disloyal by constantly correcting the other in public, breaking into each other's stories, etc.

Further Reading on This Topic

Friends and Friendships, Jerry and Mary White, NavPress.

7

What about Fun?
Remember Fun?

*I*t was Friday night. I was sitting in my special green chair, bored to death. Three times Rosemary had asked me, "What do you want to do tonight?" I responded creatively with, "I don't know. What do you want to do?" After asking each other the same question three or four times, it was too late to actually do anything. The question changed to, "What do you want to watch tonight?"

When it's husband and wife, for some reason we choose to act bored or too tired to do anything. How do I know that we actually make this choice? It's simple. If that very same night a good friend stopped by unexpectedly, we would immediately come alive. We'd be ready to do whatever he or she suggested.

We all know that we should be doing creative things together. We also know how important it is to bring humor into our marriages. Yet we get lazy. We allow ourselves to fall into a routine of boredom. The crazy thing is that we act as if we would really rather be bored than go do something.

Jack was lying across the couch reading his fishing magazine, his usual position for a Friday night. Dee knew that if she didn't do something, he would be asleep before the hour was up, and it was only 8:00 P.M. "Jack?" Dee attempted to revive him. "Becky and Steve are having a few of our friends over, and they just called to ask if we wanted to join them. Why don't we walk on over for a little while."

"Honey," Jack responded without putting down his magazine, "it's Friday, I've been with people all week, and I'm just too tired to get together with anybody. Let's just pass. I don't have it in me to be fun tonight."

Other Couples Shouldn't Make the Difference

No sooner was the word "tonight" out of Jack's mouth than the front doorbell rang. Two of the couples at the gathering down the street had come over to get them. Dee went to the door; when Jack heard her talking to his friends, he leaped off the couch. Buttoning his shirt, Jack arrived at the front door. "Are you guys coming on down to Steve's?" one of their friends asked. Before Dee could think of a proper response, Jack said, "We'll be there in about ten minutes."

Jack and Dee went to their friends' house that night and they had a great time. As they were walking home about 11:30, Jack said, "Boy, that was hilarious." To which Dee responded, "You know, you didn't want to go. If they hadn't come to get us, you would have fallen asleep on the couch before nine like you do most Friday nights." Jack chose to go and have fun because someone other than his wife asked him. It's all a choice.

For some reason spouses find it hard to have fun together unless it includes other couples. Many times the other spouses are the motivating reasons for the activity in the first place. We just don't choose to have fun with or for each other. Jack indicated he was too tired to do anything when his wife asked. When his friends asked, however, he chose to find the energy to get involved with the activity at hand.

Humor in a Marriage Is Very Important

Jack indicated that it was a time of hilarity. Including humor in the marriage relationship is very similar to including Friday-night activities. We often overlook the need for humor between husbands and wives, and yet we love to laugh with friends. One wife said she was shocked to hear one of her husband's co-workers say, "Your husband is the absolute life of the office. He's so funny he should be on a stage." That was news to her. He had had a great sense of humor when they were dating, but after a few years of marriage humor just wasn't part of their marital routine.

Many years ago Rosemary and I were very involved in a presidential campaign. Unfortunately, Rosemary was incredibly misinformed. She was supporting the wrong candidate!

I decided to help her out, so I went down to my local campaign headquarters to get an eight-by-ten glossy photo of my man. I got home before she did that evening, so I took the painting down from the wall over the couch and taped my candidate's picture there in its place. When Rosemary got home and saw it, we both had a good laugh. But that was just the beginning of her dirty-tricks campaign against *my* candidate!

Later that same night, as I got ready to go to bed, I found the picture of my man taped to the underside of the toilet seat. We roared from separate rooms, me in the bathroom and Rosemary in another room waiting for me to find him. All through that election season I would put the picture of my candidate in a place of prominence in our little apartment, only to find him later in a place of degradation.

One evening as I was pulling in from work I found myself already laughing as I got out of the car. I was trying to anticipate where she would put the picture next. Then it occurred to me how nice it was to walk in the door laughing. That little picture had brought us an amazing amount of entertainment, and it didn't cost us anything. It did cost my candidate the election, however.

Humor is a very important and yet often-missing ingredient in the marriage relationship. It's not that we are incapable of laughter; we do it with other people. It's just that as spouses we get out of the habit. We stop trying to do things that are funny when it's just the two of us. It's easier to recline on the couch.

What About Spontaneity?

It's not only that Jack thought he was too tired to get up and laugh with friends. There was something else that caused him to feel nailed to that couch. Doing something on the spur of the moment was out of his comfort zone. He had developed a Friday-night marital routine. Basically, his routine could be titled "The Journey of Choosing Boredom." To be spontaneous and do something different at the last minute was more than he could handle. Jack was nailed down to the couch and he chose not to get up.

Fifteen years ago, before we had children, Rosemary and I were sitting in the master bedroom of our new house. It was 10:00 P.M. and we were undressed for bed. Rosemary had on my favorite negligee (not much to it), and I was sitting there in only my jockey shorts. We were winding down for the night when Rosemary said, "Wouldn't you love to have a chocolate milk shake about now?"

I couldn't care less about the milk shake, but her request did give me an interesting idea. She could see something churning in my mind and asked, "What are you thinking about?"

"I've got a great idea," I began. "Let's go get a milk shake at that new Burger King on Sheridan Street!" She responded with, "It's too late and I don't want to get dressed anyway."

"No! I don't mean get dressed," I explained as she stared at me in disbelief. "Let's go as we are." Rosemary started to object, but I just kept right on talking. "We'll get in the car in the garage and buzz up the door. The car has tinted windows, so no one will see. We can go through the drive-through window and get two milk shakes, and no one will ever know."

I need to add here that Rosemary spent most of her childhood in the mission field. I'm saying that to indicate that she's very conservative and modest about the clothes she wears out in public. The whole thought of driving to Burger King with next-to-nothing on was beyond her comprehension. Actually it was to me, too, but talking her into it became a challenge!

Finally, thirty minutes later, she got tired of my badgering her and gave in. I grabbed a five-dollar bill out of my wallet, and we raced for the garage. She got into the car, but I was the only one laughing at that point.

We pulled up to the drive-through speaker box and I ordered our milk shakes. Rosemary immediately said, "Put that window back up," as if there were fifty Burger King employees hiding behind the bushes next to the speaker box! I was having a great time laughing. Boy, this is spontaneity at its best!

Pulling through the window, I got the milk shakes as Rosemary sat there staring straight ahead. She was there, but she sure wasn't going to have a good time.

We drove out of Burger King that night having done something spontaneous. It was a night we will never forget. We stepped out of our comfort zone.

Actually, we'll never forget that night because there's more to the story. As we drove down Sheridan Street back toward our house, I decided to add a little to our adventure. When I drove past the turn to our neighborhood, Rosemary gasped and asked, "What are you doing? Where do you think you're going?"

I decided that this would be a nice time to go for a drive, maybe cruise the beach here in Fort Lauderdale. Before I could make up a good response to her question, I looked in the rearview mirror and, to my horror, I saw flashing lights. I was being pulled over by the police. This was no longer fun!

I pulled off of Sheridan Street and pulled over for my encounter with the police. Rosemary looked faint and the police officer just sat in his car behind us. Several horrible things occurred to me at that moment. My underwear didn't have a pocket for a wallet. I had only grabbed money and left my license at home. It also occurred to me that this officer was waiting for me to get out of my car and walk back to him, in my jockey shorts. I'm grateful Rosemary didn't have access to a weapon that night or she would be writing this book without me.

Finally, the officer came walking up to our car, shined his flashlight in my half-opened window, and burst out laughing as I began my plea. "Officer, I know this looks strange, but I don't have my license with me. We're married. We live just around the corner there. My name is Bob Barnes. I'm the director of Sheridan House for Boys." My explanation didn't curb his laughter at all, but he did follow us back home so that I could get some pants on and come out to his car with my license.

We have since been able to laugh at this incident, even Rosemary. In fact, every time we go to Burger King we have to restrain ourselves from laughter. We're not suggesting that everyone take their clothes off and go get a milk shake. What we are suggesting is that we break the rut we're in when it comes to marital activities. Decide to be spontaneous. When one spouse suggests doing something, the other spouse needs to choose to get the energy to do it.

Pull out the nails that are holding you down to your routine or couch. Pull out the nails that have you stuck to the television. Don't wait for friends to invite you to do things that are fun. Choose to do fun things as a husband and wife. You'll be amazed how much energy you really have. You'll also be surprised how much it will mean to your marriage. One final word of advice, however: Don't go out of the house without putting your clothes on.

Summary

1. Choose to do fun activities with each other. Don't wait for friends to come and get you. Choose to find the energy.

2. Find humor again. Humor should be used to show friends and co-workers what a fun person you are. Inject humor into your marriage to bring back fun.

3. Find spontaneity. Get off the couch, away from the television, and do something that is out of your comfort zone.

4. Keep your clothes on when you leave home.

Discussion Questions

1. What about your weekly routine? Do you have times that have been set aside just for the two of you to have fun?

2. Who is the most spontaneous one in your marriage? What are some of the things that hinder each one of you from being more spontaneous (small children, tired, too many activities)? What are some ways to work around these hindrances?

3. Choose a time that you can count on when the two of you can do something alone. Try to set something for once a week.

4. Make a list of fun things you can do in your community. This list should include things that are free or inexpensive. Then add activities that are expensive for special occasions.

5. Decide when you can do something on this list. Plan to do this activity at a time when you are most in a rut, such as the Friday-night-routine time.

Further Reading on This Topic

Ten Dates for Mates, Dave and Claudia Arp, Thomas Nelson Publishers.

8

That's How Mom and Dad Did It

In the great set of instructions for a successful marriage, the Creator of the marriage relationship spoke to the issue of in-laws. "Man will leave his father and mother . . ." (Gen. 2:24 NIV) is early advice on how to think about the marriage relationship.

Is it important to think through the need to emancipate ourselves from our previous family allegiance? We are told that one of the top three reasons for divorce in our culture is conflict with in-laws (the other two are finances and the inability to communicate about the sexual relationship). It's important, but many of us don't understand the impact of our parents and in-laws.

Because we lived with our parents for the first two decades of our lives, our parents certainly have an impact on us, both positive and negative. Part of who we are and how we make decisions is affected by this first twenty years. Therefore, it's important to the success of a marriage that each couple look at the influence their parents have on them and discuss what this means to that marriage.

The Proximity Impact

Perhaps you spent the first year of your marriage in the same geographical area as both sets of parents. This fact may have had a great impact on how you handled holidays. Remember your first Thanksgiving as a married couple. You dreamed that it would be a wonderful time of finally getting to share yourselves with each other and celebrating. Instead, it turned out to be a day of meeting the expectations of two sets of parents.

All of a sudden new questions popped up. To whose house would you go to celebrate Thanksgiving? His parents wouldn't understand if you didn't show up. After all, his older brothers and sisters would be there. You'd be the only ones not there, and his mother was very insistent that you not ruin the whole day.

On the other hand, if you didn't go to her parents' house, those sweet people would once again end up on the short end of the stick. They'd be really nice and understanding about it, but they'd also be hurt. They were so understanding that they always ended up with no one coming.

Decisions had to be made. And, if you were really honest about it, you would have liked to spend that particular Thanksgiving at home alone. You tried to hint at that with his parents, but his mother was ready with a response. "Oh, that would be ridiculous. How could you cook a turkey for two people! Besides, I've already ordered a two-hundred-pound turkey, and it would just go to waste if you didn't show!"

It's hard to win and emancipate yourself when you aren't prepared ahead of time. There are questions that need to be answered before a couple can respond properly to in-laws. Couples need to sit down and talk about their feelings. I've actually heard of some couples who eat two Thanksgiving meals, one at each in-laws' house.

Who Are We Here to Please? Tell Each Other

"It just makes me furious every time his mother calls," Barbara told the counselor as they sat together in the office. "His mother gets him on the phone and all she has to say is, 'It's certainly been a long time since you've taken me out to lunch on a Sunday afternoon. I guess you're just too busy for me these days.' Once she says that Fred rearranges everything and announces that we're going to take his mother out after church."

Barbara wasn't mad about the lunch; she was upset that her husband was constantly rearranging family plans because his mother wanted to test her control. Fred's mother wanted to see if she could still make her son hop when she called.

Fred, on the other hand, didn't really care. He had learned that it was easier to flow down the area of least resistance. He didn't feel he was being controlled, he just didn't care. If his mother wanted lunch and his wife didn't say much to the contrary, why not?

Fred didn't see the signals that took place. Barbara didn't say anything; she was just in a bad mood before lunch, during lunch, and after lunch. Instead of helping Fred deal with his mother, she became another problem female in his life. Fred had spent much of his life having his mother manipulate him with bad moods and guilt, so he didn't think anything about it when his wife acted that way, too. He just thought that was the way women were. Fred had learned to ignore it.

There were several very detrimental things happening in their relationship. In-law problems brought it out, but this couple was actually causing the problem to take place. It wasn't the in-laws, but the way this couple handled the controversy surrounding the in-laws that was causing the problems.

Barbara was asked by the therapist if she had talked to Fred about how it made her feel when he rearranged his family life around his mother's phone-call requests. "I've tried to talk to him, but it doesn't work. He just fires back at me, 'What do you want me to do, ignore the fact that she's my mother?'"

In reality Barbara hadn't chosen the right times to talk to Fred. She waited until they were getting ready to go to lunch, and then she just boiled over with resentment. She told Fred that it made her furious that his mother was constantly doing things like this. This was the wrong timing and the wrong thing to say. She waited until it was too late for Fred to do anything about it.

Later, with both Fred and Barbara in the counseling room, it was a safer time to have this discussion. But this discussion could have easily taken place on their back porch, if they had decided to talk rather than attack.

Barbara needed to explain to Fred how it made her feel when his mother stepped into their lives and took control. It had nothing to do with lunch. What it really demonstrated to Barbara was that she was a low second priority in Fred's life. "Oh, that's ridiculous!" Fred exploded in frustration. "You know you're my priority!"

When you think about it, that was an interesting, yet typical, response. A wife is saying that she feels she's not a priority in her husband's life, and the husband responds by saying, "Of course you know you're the priority." Obviously there's something wrong here. How can they both be right?

She says that she doesn't *feel* like a priority the way he treats her, especially where his mother is concerned. He says that in his heart his wife is his priority. Either he's not exhibiting this in his actions, or she's misreading something.

Perceptions Can Become Reality

Barbara and Fred were each perceiving something different. Worse yet, they weren't talking about it. Barbara thought she was letting him know by her moods and sarcastic comments. Fred was just doing what he had always done. He was ignoring the problem, hoping it would go away. But perceptions need to be dealt with, not ignored.

Finally, in the counselor's office Fred said, "I didn't know that this bothered you so much. Why didn't you say something to me?" Barbara responded with, "Fred! I tried to talk to you but you just said things like, 'Barbara, what do you want me to do now? We're about to go out the door and she's sitting there waiting.'"

Both were right. Fred needed to take a stand and show to all concerned, including himself, that his marriage was a priority.

Barbara, on the other hand, had not been fair or mature in the way she was dealing with Fred about the issue. In fact, she was acting just like his mother, getting moody to get her way. Unfortunately, it wasn't working.

Face the Problem as a Team

Barbara wanted Fred to see, on his own, that his mother was trying to divide his allegiances. Fred wasn't seeing it. Instead of finding a time to talk, she just got mad. They weren't playing on the same team. It's not fair for one spouse to wait for the other one to "figure it out" alone. That kind of thinking is a waste of time and can just make everyone more angry.

Barbara needed to tell Fred how she felt. Fred had to accept the fact that even though he didn't totally understand why she felt that way, he had to deal with it. Whether he understood it or not didn't make it any less real to Barbara.

The next step was to devise a plan for correcting the problem. They decided that when Fred's mother called with a request, he would respond, "Let me get back with you, Mom. I need to talk with Barbara about that."

That was a good first step, but they also needed to spend time helping Fred think through the rest of the conversation he'd be having with his mother. When that was suggested to Fred, he got defensive. "What do you mean talk about how to respond to my mother's objections? She won't object to my talking to you first. I'll just tell her and that will be it."

At this point Barbara shined in her teamship with her husband. "Fred, that may be true. But I'm a woman. And more than that, you've often said (at not very nice times in our marriage) that I remind you of your mother. I just know I can predict her response to your telling her that you'll talk it over with me and get back to her."

Fred was wise and relinquished the point. Barbara was probably right. His mother wouldn't just let it stop there. At that point they discussed possible things his mother might say, such as, "Oh, now you have to ask permission? Who's running that house, anyway?" or "I knew it. I'm just a bother and you don't really want to spend time with me anymore."

Fred took advantage of the opportunity to hear a woman help him think through the process. As a matter of fact, Barbara had predicted perfectly. Fred's mother challenged his leadership by asking him who ran his house, him or Barbara. Fred responded with, "Mom, Barbara's my wife, and we are working at making all decisions together."

One particular time there was something else that Barbara really wanted to do, and Fred had to call back and tell his mom that they wouldn't be able to be together. Fred's mother responded with a comment about Barbara that was not very nice. "Mom, you're talking about my wife. I can't sit here on the phone and listen to something like this. I'll talk to you later."

This was the beginning of Fred's emancipation from his previous family. It was the beginning of Barbara believing she was a priority. It was also the beginning of the painful process Fred's mother had to go through to realize that Fred would no longer be manipulated. It was a great beginning for all of them.

Later, Fred was able to say, "You know what? Barbara actually invited my mom over for her birthday. Before I could even say anything, I found out that my mom was coming over."

"Of course I did, Fred," Barbara cut into the conversation. "Now I'm beginning to feel secure enough in our relationship to interact with your mom. Even if she tries to pull a power move I'm confident in where I stand as far as you are concerned."

Fred now realized that he was the deterrent to his wife and mother getting to know each other. When God said, "Leave your father and mother . . ." He had a reason. The marriage is to become the priority. It needs to be obvious to all concerned.

Long-Distance In-law Impact

An interesting thing had taken place in Fred's thought process. This was one of the reasons that Fred handled the situation the way he did. He grew up in the home of a woman who manipulated to get power, and he assumed that all women did that. He just thought that was the way it was.

We bring many attitudes to the marriage relationship—attitudes, thoughts, or ways of doing things that we saw in our own homes as we grew up. After seeing things one way for two decades, we naturally begin to think that this is the way everybody does it.

One of the most important areas affected is in defining the roles of husband and wife. Everyone comes to the marriage with a different understanding of what it means to be a husband and what it means to be a wife. Roles will be discussed at length in a later chapter, but there are some surface areas that need to be looked at here.

I grew up in a home where there were no gendered chores. Everyone, male and female, pitched in and did whatever needed to be done. It wasn't that I thought I could clean something better or do the laundry faster, it was simply that I was taught that the chores weren't done until everyone's chores were done. You did whatever was left to do. That meant that the dishes were often done by the boys.

Rosemary, on the other hand, grew up in a Danish home where the husband never entered the kitchen. Anything considered domestic was not to be done by the man in the house. That's partially ethnic and partially that whole generation.

It did cause some conflicts for us when we got married. The fact that I often grabbed the laundry and did it made her feel as if I thought she was incompetent. I couldn't understand why she felt that way. I was only trying to help.

When Rosemary's parents came to visit us during those early years of our marriage we would all be sitting in the living room, talking, and I'd get up to get myself a cup of coffee. Rosemary's father would then say, "Rosemary, I'd like a cup of coffee, please." He was polite with his request, and it was what he had always done. Yet I'd find myself wanting to say, "What's the matter, are your legs broken?"

We had two ways of looking at things. One way wasn't wrong and the other right. But we didn't talk about it as a husband and wife. Instead, I just resented him and the way she served him. He wasn't wrong. He was just being himself. Rosemary and I were wrong because we weren't talking to each other.

A Previous Family of One: Dangerous

I used to think that this passage of "Leave your father and mother . . ." had nothing to do with me. I didn't have to work at emancipating myself from my previous family. I had lived alone for several years before I got married. I didn't really have a previous family.

Wrong! I had many things to look at. The family I had lived with prior to marriage was the most dangerous family of all—a family of one. A family of one doesn't have to live in routine. You eat whenever you want to and do whatever you want to. You're not responsible to anyone else.

During that first year of marriage I would call home at 4:40 in the afternoon and announce, "I won't be home for dinner. I'm playing racquetball." Just like I'd always done before I was married. It wasn't my mother who was calling, it was my own self-centeredness.

Living alone before marriage does not preclude this need to emancipate from the past family. Whether it's the in-laws or just a self-centered lifestyle of being responsible to no one but oneself, it all needs to be looked at and talked about.

Isn't There Anything Good?

One could read this chapter and decide that there's nothing good that can be brought into it from our previous families.

Nothing could be further from the truth. Each of us brings a wealth of traditions and other qualities from our homes. These are beautiful benefits that can bless our marriages.

Rosemary's family celebrates the whole Christmas season rather than just a day. It has been a blessing to our marriage. The fact that her parents instilled in her the fun of family traditions means we are able to include in our marriage many exciting ways to enjoy our own family times together. It's just a matter of sorting it all out. These are blessings that must be discussed and perhaps reshaped to fit the needs of the new family.

In 1973 Rosemary and I decided to spend some time traveling through Europe. As mentioned before, we didn't have much money, so we were going to travel on the rail system. That meant we were going to take only one suitcase. It was decided that I would carry the one suitcase during this vacation.

We bought the suitcase, and as we got closer and closer to the date of departure, we began to build little piles of clothes. In one end of our bedroom I began to stack a few pairs of pants, some underwear, and shirts. Not much, really. On the other side of the bedroom, however, I noticed this massive mountain of items being stacked up. It was almost too much for the room, let alone a suitcase. I remember thinking, *What in the world is she doing? A semitrailer couldn't hold all those things!*

It just wouldn't all fit into our suitcase. We had to talk about what would fit and get rid of the extra baggage. That's the key. There are many great things we bring into a marriage from our previous experiences. Some things fit; some things don't. It just causes more difficulties if you avoid discussing these issues. Trying to fit them all in puts undo strain on the hinges. Take advantage of using the great things you each bring into the marriage and get rid of the extra baggage. Take the time and talk.

Summary

1. Each married couple needs to be open about discussing the impact their in-laws have on the marriage.

2. It's important to let spouses and in-laws understand what the priority relationship is.

3. It's necessary to be willing to discuss the attitudes each marriage partner brings to the marriage—the ones that were created in the homes where they grew up.

4. In-laws can have a tremendous impact from thousands of miles away.

5. Whether it's true or not, your spouse may perceive that he or she is not as important to you as your parents are.

6. A previous family of one can be dangerous.

7. Take time to sort out the baggage.

Discussion Questions

1. List some enriching traditions and ideas each of you has brought to your marriage from your families. Which ones have you implemented into your own home? Which ones have you left out? Why?

2. List marital attitudes that each of you has brought with you from the homes you grew up in. Include roles, things you expect your spouse to do, and methods for solving problems.

3. In what areas do your in-laws enhance your marriage? In what ways do they hinder it?

4. What are some practical steps that you can take to help your spouse feel like the priority in your life?

5. Is there anything that your spouse does to make you feel like he or she still considers his or her parents the priority?

9

The New In-law Factor

As if the in-law factors of old weren't difficult enough to deal with, now we have additional ones. The effects in-laws have on a marriage have always been dramatic. That's why the original description of marriage, in the second chapter of Genesis, instructed us to leave our fathers and mothers. Today's culture adds a new dimension, or maybe we should say new pressures, to the marriage.

Take, for instance, the ethnic factor. When Hurricane Andrew pounded south Florida in August of 1992, many homes were destroyed. Overnight, eighty-five thousand families were without homes. Overnight, relatives of those families had to decide the best way to help.

South Florida has many cross-cultural marriages. There are many couples where an Anglo is married to a Hispanic. This can lead to problems, especially when it comes to the impact of the in-laws.

When the hurricane hit, homes were opened to those who were without a place to live. Everyone knew that this was necessary. However, after a month or so, it became a difficulty. The families began to see that the situation was going to last much longer—maybe even a year or more.

George and Maria came to see a counselor when they couldn't take it any longer. "I suggested we come here so we could at least have a place to talk in private," George started, only half kidding. The hurricane had destroyed the homes of Maria's parents and of her brother's family. The day after the hurricane her family arrived on her doorstep. It was the natural thing to do, if you're Hispanic. Maria's parents moved in, and her father assumed the leadership of the house. To this older gentleman, he wasn't being difficult—that's the way his culture did things.

That worked for a day or two, and then George started to go crazy. What had happened to his home? He didn't want to offend his in-laws, but he couldn't even stand coming home any longer.

Was George wrong and Maria's family right? Or was it vice versa? Actually, neither was right or wrong. They came from different cultures, and that was impacting their marriage. When they sat in the counselor's office they realized two things. George once again realized that Maria's parents really didn't have any place else they could live. They also realized that George couldn't live this way any longer. It began to seem as if their situation was beyond help.

The one ingredient they were missing was communication. They needed to talk to each other; they needed to have a family meeting. Otherwise, George was going to end up acting like he was antisocial by not interacting well with the rest of the family. They had to decide a better way for them to be able to exist in George and Maria's home. They definitely needed a family meeting.

Other situations have more tangible answers, however. Living in a place like south Florida means that many relatives like to take advantage of the opportunity to visit this tourist spot (and get free lodging). One young wife said to me, "In my family it's just an accepted fact that when relatives are passing through town or in town for any reason that they should stay with you. In fact, they really don't even need to call ahead. It's accepted that they just arrive on your doorstep."

That may have been the way her culture, her ethnic group, functioned, but it certainly wasn't part of her husband's background. Her husband was raised in the northeast where people are much more private and isolated. For the first four years of their marriage they had a family member of hers stay with them at least once a month. Her husband had had it. He was trying to be gracious, but now her two aunts had written to say they wanted to come to Florida and stay with them for a couple of weeks. This brought the whole difficulty to a head. The husband was ready for a break from all the relatives; he didn't want to be "invaded" anymore by her family.

"What can I do? It would be an incredible insult to call my aunts and tell them they can't come. If I told them it was because we were on overload from visitors, it would circulate throughout my whole family. They'll either think that we are rude or that we're having marital problems. My husband just doesn't understand!"

This is most certainly a case where the Genesis 2 principle comes into play. Which ethnic tradition was best for the marriage? No visitors? The total open-door policy that does not offend extended family members? Or a variation of that policy that would make the marriage a priority?

In this particular case they talked about it and realized that a tough phone call had to be made. For the sake of their marriage, this young lady needed to tell her aunts that this was not a good time to visit and stay with them. How the aunts received this news was their own business. It would be better to have them talk about her now rather than continue to put more strain on the marriage so that they would really have something to talk about later.

When two very different ethnic groups come together in marriage it is mandatory that each spouse protect the other from any sort of "ethnic abuse." It just may save a marriage.

"I'm Desperate for a Loan"

Jack kept getting phone calls from his brother, who was having trouble in business. Jack was doing all right with his finances, but his brother Bill was buried by debt. Time and time again he was borrowing money from Jack.

At first it wasn't much money, but after a while it built up to a couple of thousand dollars. Bill kept saying that he was going to pay it back, but he never did. He just kept asking Jack for more.

One Saturday afternoon Bill came over to Jack's house and said he had something personal to talk about. Obviously, he needed more money.

Taking her cue, Jack's wife, Bernice, got up from the kitchen table to leave, but this time her husband stopped her. "I think you should stay here, Honey," Jack said to his wife. So she sat back down.

Bill was shocked. In the past he had gotten his brother alone and then asked for money. This caught him off guard and he acted offended by his brother's invasion of their privacy. He got up from the table and said he'd talk to his brother later.

"Why did you do that?" Bernice asked her husband. "Bill won't understand this because finances have always been a 'men only' topic in our family," Jack responded. "Women were never included in the decisions. He had been coming to me for loans and never paying them back. This time I wanted to show him that this was your money he was taking also. I can no longer make these loans without him talking to both of us together."

This move on Jack's part had a major impact on their relationship. The fact that Jack's brother was constantly taking money from them was bad enough. The fact that Bill tried to do it behind her back made her furious. She knew the dilemma her husband was in. There had been times when Bill really did need help. But he never paid it back, and he was taking advantage of the fact that Jack and Bernice were doing well. Of course, the rest of Jack's family would now hear how Jack was tied to his wife's apron strings. It didn't matter to Jack, though. He had realized that he had to put his marriage first.

Extended families can get into bad habits if they're not careful. They can easily abuse a more successful relative and hurt his marriage. It's up to the couple to decide to make all financial decisions together. It's also up to them to decide how much is enough. Together they are better suited to make an objective decision.

Now That We're Parenting Our Parents

This is the first generation where such a large number of us will be required to take care of our parents. They're growing older, and they are going to need more assistance from their own children than ever before. This can be a terrific burden to a marriage.

For the past two generations couples have been having less children. Quite often an only child is called on to take care of an aging parent. In most cases this is the best, if not the only, option. This is where communication is mandatory.

"Where?" one husband in this situation almost screamed at me. "Where do you expect us to talk? My mother-in-law lives in our postage-stamp house and there's nowhere to go. If we move into the living room she follows us in. She's making me crazy."

"Where" might mean out of the house. Go for a walk each evening for thirty minutes, or go get a cup of coffee. If the situation is such that it can't be changed, then the couple must change the way they handle the situation.

The couple in this situation must decide that they are going to make it a priority to find somewhere to talk. This should be done a couple of times a week. "But when we go my mom tries to make us feel guilty. She says things like, 'Is there something wrong with me that you don't take me with you?' or 'I must be awfully bad for you to have to get out of the house twice a week.'" The couple has to decide that this time together is so important that nothing, not even a mother-in-law's comment, will stop it.

Second, when you do get out together, allow enough time to talk—to really talk. To really talk, you need to be able to state how you feel about the situation and how to deal with it.

Spend enough time so you get past the arguments. Spend time listening to the dilemma your partner faces. He feels invaded. She feels trapped because it's her mother, and though there's nothing she can do, she feels guilty about imposing on her husband. It's a time to listen to the other person's pain.

In these times of talking, decide on a plan to make life more bearable. One couple decided they would announce to her mother that their bedroom was off-limits—they needed their own place in the house. Yes, the mother-in-law was offended, but as time went on she realized that it improved the way her son-in-law treated her. Having his own space made him more comfortable in his own home. Prior to that, he said, "Every time I would pull into the driveway I would immediately get into a bad mood. Now at least I know where I can go to be alone."

The key to the success in handling the negative side of being able to help our parents is to keep the lines of communication opened. Husbands and wives must keep talking rather than keep it inside. Then they must develop a plan to make the most of the situation. And they must boldly, yet lovingly, present the plan to the parent. The couple must act as one as they search for the best way to love the parent in need while balancing their need for privacy. If not, the marriage may be damaged, and the in-law will only feel more guilty.

New In-law Challenges Every Day

As we enter the next century there will be newer, yet-unthought-of challenges coming from extended families. For example, stepparent families come with all kinds of configurations, and the dilemmas just can't be anticipated. The most significant factor is that the couple decide that they will not let the sun go down on their anger. When there's a problem or something that is annoying, it is mandatory that the couple decide to devote significant time discussing the situation. If that's done regularly it can help prevent difficulties. The rule of thumb, "to leave his mother and father" means the marriage must take priority over the extended family.

Summary

1. There is an ethnic factor that can be damaging to the marriage. Differences in ethnic ideas about the marriage relationship must be dealt with.

2. Financial decisions, or any other decision to give up something for an extended family member, must be discussed by a couple. A couple should decide to operate as one person or one corporation. The partners must make the decision together before loaning money to a brother.

3. The fact that our parents are living longer is a blessing. The fact that they may need to move in with us is an opportunity that must be dealt with daily. When a parent comes to live with you, decide that there will still be private space and honest discussions.

4. Keep the lines of communication open where the extended family is concerned. Everyone has different ideas about what is and is not acceptable.

Discussion Questions

1. What are the differences between your two backgrounds that are causing conflicts in your marriage? What is the most practical way to resolve them?

2. What are the pressures that you feel coming from your extended families?

3. What are some practical ways to show your spouse that your marriage is a priority in these situations?

Part 3

The Communication Process

10

Now How Could That Hurt Her Feelings?

Mystery #1: It was 1972, our first year of marriage. While Rosemary was getting dressed up so that we could go out to eat, I was waiting for her on the couch. When she finished dressing, this new wife of mine stepped into the living room of our tiny apartment and asked, "Well, how do I look?"

I glanced up from my magazine and responded with, "You look nice. Are you ready to go?"

"You look nice," was a very positive statement as far as I was concerned. From Rosemary's perspective, however, if this was all the response she got out of me, she might as well have not wasted her time. "Nice. That's all you have to say?" She didn't actually say that verbally, but I could read it on her face.

There was a problem here. "Nice" was a big word to me. Nice was nothing to her. But it didn't stop there.

Mystery #2: We went out to dinner that night, and it was not a particularly spectacular evening. When we got home I turned on the television, and we sat on the couch together. At the first commercial I turned to her and said, "Obviously, something is wrong. Do you want to talk about it?" At this point we began to talk, but a problem arose—the commercial only lasted about three minutes. It didn't seem unreasonable for me to ask if we could continue this discussion at the next commercial.

I turned my attention back to the television show without waiting for her response. At the next commercial I turned to talk to her. To my surprise, Rosemary was gone! There just wasn't any place a person could go to hide in this little apartment, so I was surprised that I didn't see her anywhere.

I looked across the room and noticed that the bedroom door was closed. I walked to the door and opened it; the light was off. When I turned on the light I found my wife sitting in the middle of the bed crying. The most logical thing for me to do at that point seemed to be to ask a diagnostic question. "Rosemary, what's the matter?"

This may have seemed logical to me, but apparently she didn't think so. When I asked her what was wrong, she responded with an answer that any man married over a month can remember hearing. Rosemary responded, while weeping, "Nothing!" I asked the same question several times only to receive the same response.

That was very confusing. Why would somebody sit in the middle of a bed and weep if there was nothing wrong? I'd never encountered anything like that. None of the guys on the football team or at the racquetball courts ever did that. Was I supposed to get something out of this coded message? Or was I supposed to dial 911 for psychiatric assistance?

We Talk at Different Levels

Rosemary was trying to tell me that she wanted to talk and she wanted to tell me what was wrong, but it couldn't be done during a three-minute commercial. And wasn't our time of talking more important than a television program anyway? My thought was that if that's what she wanted to say, then why didn't she say so? Perhaps she knew that I wouldn't respond to that too well. Or perhaps she had tried to say that by her behavior and I just went right on watching television. Whatever the reason, it became very obvious that we often talk at different levels.

Men often talk in three-minute, fix-it type intervals. Express an opinion and that's it. Women often talk at a much deeper level. They express an opinion and then wrap it in feelings. They seem to be much more adept at the science of communication.

My wife is able to get into a deep conversation about personal things while she's still pulling up the chair to sit down. I can't do that. I find it difficult to express my feelings about things. The times I do attempt to talk about these things, it takes me much longer to work up to that point. It's just easier to talk about solutions than feelings.

In high school Rosemary talked to her friends for hours. They talked about who hurt whose feelings. They talked about relationships. In high school I talked on the phone for two minutes. I only wanted to know who won the game. Once I got the score and the details, what else was there to talk about? How I felt about the game? No. That didn't make sense.

This was beautifully illustrated by our Sunday school classes one day. Rosemary teaches a class of a dozen ladies. In another room, I teach their husbands. One Sunday, when the class was letting out, I noticed that the ladies in her class were walking out of their room with tears in their eyes. Some were even hugging. My men, on the other hand, were slapping each other on the back and making fun of each other as they left for the church service. Wow, there was really an obvious difference in the intimacy level between these two classes. Rosemary's ladies seemed much closer to each other than did the men in my class.

At lunch that afternoon I asked Rosemary about her class. "What do you do in there that causes those ladies to feel so close?" My wife responded with, "We spend time praying together." I was a little insulted by her answer! As if we never prayed in the men's class!

"What do you mean you pray together? Of course you pray in Sunday school! So do we!" I responded, a little put out by her insinuation that we didn't pray.

Rosemary told me that the ladies in her class asked the other ladies to pray about personal things, including various aspects of their marriages. As she told me about some of the things that the ladies were sharing, I realized that there was certainly a difference in the intimacy level of the two classes. When the men in my class mentioned prayer requests it never had anything to do with themselves. They would mention things such as, "Pray for this guy at work . . . I don't remember his name, but his wife has cancer." Another prayer request might be, "Pray for one of the guys who works for my uncle back in Kansas. The man got hurt on the job."

Everything they said was far from personal and far from a feeling level. The men just found it difficult to share or talk at an intimate level. Intimacy is something the man in this culture is not taught to talk about. Yet the woman is very sophisticated in her ability to discuss things at a deep, feeling level.

One afternoon as I walked into my house, I noticed the car belonging to a friend of Rosemary's was parked out front. Walking through the kitchen, I found Rosemary and her friend sitting at the table, both in tears. Later, after her friend left, I asked my wife, "How long had Linda been there before I came in?" "Oh, I guess about ten minutes," was Rosemary's reply.

Ten minutes and they were already in tears! That's incredible! I could sit there for ten hours and not get to that level.

One of the problems that plagues a marriage is the fact that the marriage partners talk to each other on different levels. She is intending to talk on one level (this is how I feel), and he is intending to talk on another level (this is how we can fix this . . . in a hurry). She wants to relate, and he wants to fix the problem just as quickly as he can.

This is all very confusing, because it wasn't that way when the couple was dating. At least it didn't seem that way. When they were dating they would sit in front of her dorm for hours and just talk. She saw that he was a wonderful conversationalist. He seemed to talk just for the sake of talking.

In reality, he was talking because he knew that was what she wanted to do. He probably didn't even know it. He was trying to win her heart, and that meant relating to her. His conversations were ultimately heading toward one goal . . .

marriage (or something more devious). He was trying to make "the sale." Once they got married, and he made "the sale," it was hard for him to see why they should still sit and talk for hours. After all, "the sale" was made, why should he have to "service the account?"

Levels of Communication

Communication is the level of intimacy at which a person is willing or able to talk. Problems arise when spouses talk to each other at different levels of intimacy. The husband's talking about how the food tasted at the restaurant and how it is a great meal at a great price. The wife's talking about how she felt at the restaurant and the fact that it was so loud that they didn't get much of a chance to talk. She didn't feel it was much of a date. He thought it was a great time. They were both looking at the event from different levels or approaches.

The Grunt Level

The most shallow level of communication, if it can be considered communication at all, can be called the grunt level. It is an obligatory response to make verbal contact with another person. Teenagers have perfected this level to an art. When a parent asks a teenager how school was that particular day, the response is a grunt that says nothing.

Parent: How was school today, son?

Teenager: Fine.

Parent: What did you do?

Teenager: Nothing.

With that the conversation ends. The amazing thing is that the parent accepts that as actually talking to the child—nothing really took place. It was a form of obligatory communication.

Many couples deal at this level as they see each other for the first time each evening. "How was work today?" "Fine." As a culture we have gotten into the habit of grunting at people without listening to what they say in response. You pass a person in the office and give the obligatory grunt of, "Hi! How ya doin'?" Instead of the accepted cultural response of "Fine," suppose the person said, "I'm near suicidal." We'd never hear them! We're so accustomed to these grunts that we'd just respond without really hearing what our suicidal friend said. So we'd answer, "That's great! Good to see you." Then we'd walk on by as if we never really even saw the person.

This grunt level is the way many spouses interact with each other. They just say the required things to each other and never really listen. After a while they don't even know each other anymore.

Journalist Level

At the second level of communication is the person who is full of information about the people and events around him. When talking with his spouse he can vehemently express his opinion about others and what they are doing. Unfortunately, he rarely talks about anything other than the facts and his opinions about these facts.

One woman in my office said that she had been married to her husband for seven years and realized that she didn't know much of anything about him. "I knew his opinions about other people, politics, the church, just about everything. But it stops there. I don't really know who he is."

The male gender is taught by our culture to have an opinion about everything. They're taught to even have opinions about things they don't know anything about. Having an opinion and sticking to that opinion protects the male from having to talk at a deeper level.

This lady's husband thought about what he had heard her say and responded with an interesting comment. "I just thought

I was supposed to have opinions about things. The more I thought about it, the more I realized that having an opinion would mean that I wouldn't have to discuss the subject. It was as if I was saying, 'There! There's my opinion! Now we can move on to other things since this is so black and white to me.'"

Why would there need to be a discussion with someone who was so opinionated about the topic? This journalist level is really the level that the Western culture male has been taught to hide behind. Men generally know how to express opinions and state the facts as they see them but they don't know how to go any deeper.

Typically, the woman in the marriage is capable of going into the next level of communication, while the man has been taught to hover at this journalist level. Often he uses opinions as a guard to keep himself from having to communicate at an intimate level.

In our own marriage I can remember Rosemary saying to me, "Could we just sit out on the porch and talk tonight?" My response would be, "What do you want to talk about?" I wanted to get my opinions ready. But then she would baffle me with statements like, "I don't want to talk about anything in particular, I just want to talk."

It was hard for me to imagine doing that. I thought talking was reserved for opinions or for fixing things. She didn't want my quick solutions. Instead, she wanted a relationship where we would sit and share feelings. That was a very difficult bridge for me to cross. To step beyond talking about my opinions about the world around us and talk about how things made me feel was a bridge that seemed foggy and uncrossable. As a male I couldn't see how you could talk about feelings and ever know when you arrived at the end of the conversation. At least when a person talks about opinions, or offers solutions to problems, it's easy to know when you've arrived at the end of the road.

It's a big bridge between level two, the journalist level of facts and opinions, and level three, the feelings level, but it's a bridge that must be crossed. In many marriages one person,

usually the wife, is sitting on the other side of that bridge waiting for her spouse to cross over. They are both very lonely because of the gulf between these two levels.

Feelings Level

In chapter 6 we talked about a pro football player who suf-
fered an injury that took him out of the action for several
weeks. When he returned to the field, everyone knew where he
was hurt, where he would be vulnerable. It's a real risk. The
knee that has been operated on or the shoulder that has been
injured can become a target for the other team.

Becky and Mike were trying to do a good job as parents to
their two children. One night, while they were going for a
drive, they had a great discussion about their progress as parents. After more than an hour of discussing the things they
needed to do, Mike risked revealing his feelings about this
whole project of parenting. He revealed a weakness.

"Becky," Mike began while looking straight ahead at the
road, "you grew up in the kind of home where your parents did
these things. Your dad led the family in devotions and reading
the Bible. I never saw it done, so it's a little awkward for me to
do. I know I'm supposed to do these things and I want to. I
guess I just don't know how."

For Mike to say that he didn't know how to do anything
was a real step over the bridge. That night as they talked Mike
went on to risk talking about how he felt so inadequate for the
task of parenting and yet how much he loved his family. He
told Becky that he wanted to be a spiritual leader in his home,
but that he needed her help. Mike stepped over into the beginning of level three.

Level three can't be entered into lightly. When a person
begins to share about weaknesses this is an intimacy that must
be protected. Like with the injured football player, when these
areas of weakness are revealed, they can be exploited and cause
great harm.

A couple of weeks after Becky and Mike had their significant talk in the car, Becky was having a horrible day with the children. They were wild and disobedient just as Mike walked in the door. The first thing out of his mouth was an unfair criticism of the way she was handling the situation. At that point Becky lost it. She turned around and fired back at Mike with, "If you were the dad that you talk about being, I wouldn't be having these problems!"

It was an unfair shot at a vulnerable area that Mike had chosen to reveal, and it struck a deep blow. It was awhile before Mike was able to trust Becky with another level three form of communication.

Level three goes beyond opinions and solutions. It is a venture into a new form of relationship. It is a sharing of what a person really feels about the relationship. Level three, at its best, is reached when one person feels safe enough to share areas of weakness or feelings that may appear to be weak.

One time, about four years after our marriage, Rosemary and I were sitting in a restaurant, talking. Somehow we began talking about how we differ in our opinions of what it is to be romantic. Rosemary said to me, "You think romantic is a preamble to sex. It wouldn't be romantic to you if we didn't make love somewhere in close proximity to a time of romance."

I was shocked! What is it to be romantic if sex isn't involved? My basic response to her statement was, "You mean it's not?" As we talked, it became very apparent that I had no idea what she meant when she used the word *romance*. We had very different definitions of the feeling or mood called romance. Flippantly, I admitted to her, "I give up. Obviously I don't know what you mean by my being romantic! Should I unbutton my shirt down to my navel, get a big gold chain necklace, and splash on some cologne?" I was trying, in a very guarded way, to admit that I didn't understand how I could meet this need she had for romance.

As we talked further I realized, for the first time in our marriage, that it was okay to say I didn't know how to do something. It was okay to admit weakness. It was okay to ask for help. It was even okay to enter into a discussion of something that she could guide me in. I had been so insecure in who I was and in our relationship that I found it difficult to admit weakness. Yet I desperately needed to be able to reveal who I was. Without realizing it, I yearned for the opportunity to share at this level.

This third level exemplifies what is meant in the Genesis 2 definition of marriage, which includes the phrase "naked and not ashamed." A marriage partner is someone with whom you share your innermost thoughts and yet do not feel ashamed to let that person know your vulnerabilities. This is a very real need in our lives, and the lack of this intimacy can cause significant problems.

So many people get married and never experience this level-three communication, and they become vulnerable to problems. For the past eighteen years I have heard the same discussion repeated over and over in one form or another: "I don't really know how it all got started. I met her at the office and we went out to lunch. Somehow we were able to talk at a deeper level than I ever experienced with my wife. Before I knew it we were having an affair."

Many people involved in affairs don't realize that they aren't having an affair with another person. Instead, they are lured by this unmet need for level-three communication. They yearn to fill that need for someone to communicate with at an intimate level. They get trapped by "naked and not ashamed," outside their marriage relationship. The difference here is that they *are* ashamed.

Level-three communication, where intimacy and feelings are discussed freely, is a growing relationship. It doesn't just happen all at once. It takes a long time. It is a necessary bridge to cross, so that two can become one. As one wife put it, "I got married expecting to spend a life growing closer and closer to Bill. But he got married and that was it. He didn't seem to want to get close to me once we were married."

It's not so much a matter of not wanting as it is a matter of not knowing how. Most men are not naturally able to sit down and talk at a feeling level. They haven't been taught how. They have no experience practicing this. And there aren't any instruction manuals to read to make it easy. It's a risk to step across a new bridge. But it's a risk worth taking.

Summary

1. As husbands and wives we often carry on conversations, but at different levels of communication. It's difficult to have a meaningful relationship when we are constantly communicating at different levels.

2. The first level of communication that we all understand well is the grunt level. We respond with obligatory words directed toward the people in our lives.

3. The second level of communication is the journalist level. We often keep people from knowing who we are by listing facts and expressing opinions about the things around us, but never really talking about ourselves. This is the level where most males stay.

4. The deepest level of communication is the feelings level. This is where we risk opening up and sharing at a naked level. We risk talking about feelings and inadequacies. We risk letting our partners know we are vulnerable.

5. It is hard for both husbands and wives to get to level three, but a goal of the marriage process is to have another person to share with at this deep and secure level.

Discussion Questions

1. What level do you generally communicate on with others? With your spouse?

2. On what level do you think your spouse generally communicates with others? With you?

3. Is level-three communication a regular part of your relationship? Do you communicate at this level weekly? Monthly? Ever?

4. What keeps you from communicating at level three? What hinders your communication? What enhances it?

5. If you are able to communicate at level three with someone else, what makes you free to share at that level with him or her? How can you incorporate that ingredient into your marriage?

11

Procedure Setting

Part three of this book is titled The Communication Process, and that's exactly what it is. For some reason the dating process leads us to believe that we will be able to sit out front on the porch talking forever. But that's not necessarily true. There is a process involved in marital communication. Part of that communication process is actually deciding to communicate after the wedding. This happens when a couple makes the decision to establish some procedures that will allow them to communicate.

"Set some procedures? You've got to be kidding!" I will never forget the young wife who said that. She was sitting in my office when I suggested that she and her husband establish communication procedures. "That's ridiculous," she began. "You make it sound so mechanical and unromantic. The last thing I want Billy to do is put me on his calendar so we can talk."

It does sound unromantic. This young wife was waiting for a spontaneous moment when they could come together one evening and just sit and talk for hours.

She had already waited for three years for this "spontaneous moment" to take place. I asked her how much longer she wanted to wait.

Procedure #1

Billy looked his wife in the eye at that meeting in my office and said, "You know, he's right. We would wait to do this forever. At the office, when I need to talk to the staff, we set a time for a staff meeting." "But I'm not your staff," Donna angrily cut in. Billy continued with, "I know you're not my staff. And I know that I need to take my talking time with you even more seriously than my talking with my staff. I put the things I take seriously on my calendar. The things that aren't that important I can just wait until I get around to it. If ever!"

Well said. Their "if ever" hadn't happened yet. Donna had the emotional need to communicate with her husband. He had the need to make this an important part of his life. In order to make this an important date Billy understood the need to put talking on his calendar. He had to set some procedures.

The first step toward better communication is to acknowledge the fact that procedures are necessary. Regardless of the fact that it may seem unromantic or forced, the bottom line is that it may never happen if it isn't planned.

"Why?" one woman asked. "My grandparents didn't need to have procedures for communicating. They just seemed to sit together and talk."

That was all well and good for people of your grandparents' time, or for the Waltons and their idealized television family. Yesterday's couples didn't need to plan ahead for who's going to take the kids to soccer practice and who's going to pick them up either. The fact that they didn't need to plan time to communicate doesn't mean that we shouldn't plan. This is a different time with different demands. We need to adjust to the fact that we must be wiser about protecting our family time.

If a couple doesn't protect their own marriage, no one else will. If I don't put my family into my calendar, my calendar will end up getting filled with meetings and obligations. My family will only get the holes in my schedule, the junk time nobody else wants. My family and my marriage are more important than that. So we need to acknowledge the need for marital communication procedures.

Procedure #2

Put the date to communicate into the calendar. This is not as easy as it sounds. There are many things to take into consideration when setting the date to talk.

1. How much time should you set aside? In order to get to a level of communication where feelings and deep thoughts can be expressed, level three, a significant amount of time must be allotted. A good place to start is an hour and a half.

"So long? Who has an hour and a half just sitting empty in his life?" I have heard this sentiment many times. My response is always the same. "When is the last time you watched a ball game on television, sat and watched a video, or had a long lunch with a friend or associate? Somehow you made the time." If it's important, we seem to be able to carve out the time.

To start, the husband and wife should decide that they will carve out that hour and a half each week to talk. But that isn't enough. It also has to be the right hour and a half.

2. What is your best time of day to communicate? Most of us can't cut a block out of the middle of the day. Some couples who don't successfully schedule these times together end up trying to talk at bedtime. Often this is a good time for one spouse, but the worst possible time for the other.

Many times spouses function on different biological time clocks. When we were first married, Rosemary believed that the time to get involved in deep discussions was when we went to bed. She is a night person. I'm a morning person. Going to bed at the end of the day stimulates Rosemary to talk. Going to bed brings to my mind only two thoughts, and neither of those has to do with in-depth communication!

We would put our heads on the pillow, reach over to turn out the lights, and Rosemary would then launch into some incredible conversation. In seconds I would respond with "Zzzzzz." She would be furious, as if I had intentionally insulted her. We quickly realized that our best time for communication was not late at night.

We also discovered that first thing in the evening when we got home from work was not a good time for us to talk either. I can't walk into the house and immediately launch into an in-depth conversation. The fact that my body has arrived home does not necessarily mean that my brain has arrived! My brain is usually a few miles behind me and will catch up later. That's why I like to go through my "coming home" routine that includes looking through the mail, emptying my pockets, and petting the dog. It gives my brain an opportunity to catch up.

Everyone's best communication time is different, and it will take a blending of the schedules to find the best time for you as a couple. You will probably also have to sacrifice the television set that one night.

Procedure #3

When we go into a staff meeting at Sheridan House we know that it is important enough that we don't want to be interrupted. Rather than have various staff members get up and down and break the concentration, we do two things. We take every phone in our administrative building off the hook. We also close the door, which lets everyone know that we are in an important meeting.

It's interesting that we are willing to do that at work, yet few people seem willing to do that at home. Communication at home is far more significant, but we have not been trained to believe that.

1. Deal with the phones. Either take them off the hook or, if life will absolutely stop when you miss a phone call, invest in an answering machine. That way you can screen your calls.

Using an answering machine when you are actually home

doesn't mean you're being deceptive. It means you are counting your family time as precious and you don't want to be interrupted—especially by salespeople. Our phone message actually says we're home but unable to talk at the moment.

It sometimes makes Rosemary crazy, but I don't even answer the door when we're spending time as a family. If we have set aside a time to be together, as a couple or a family, and someone chooses that time to knock on my front door without calling first, I just don't answer the door. That makes a real statement to my children. By not answering the door I show them that my time with them is too valuable to be interrupted.

I do that at the office. If someone stops by to see me when I am counseling with a family, I don't interrupt my time with that family, who had scheduled an appointment, to see this impromptu visitor. It's not fair to the people with scheduled appointments.

And if that's true at the office, it's even more true at home. At least my children feel special when I do it. I'm not always sure Rosemary agrees! She thinks it borders on being rude. Perhaps I'm using it as an excuse to have fun being rude. Whatever the motivation, conscious or subconscious, we need to protect our family appointments. Guard against the intruders into family time: television, phone, and front door.

2. Deal with the kids. Another privacy invader that is often not seen as an intruder is the children. Young children don't always understand that mom and dad need some time alone. In fact, they seem to enjoy bursting into that time and playing for the center stage. We will all be better parents if we can take some time away from parenting to have a "staff meeting." When the children are young, one answer to the dilemma may be to get a baby-sitter. This keeps the children, especially small children, occupied and safe while you spend uninterrupted time talking.

Procedure #4

The final component of procedure setting is the location of the staff meeting. The Sheridan House administrative building has two conference or meeting rooms. One seats twenty people around a long table; the other seats eighty people in front of a big fireplace. Other organizations and churches are constantly calling us to use these rooms for their staff meetings. Why? It's not because they don't have their own places to meet. It's because these places offer them an opportunity to get away from the routine and their own busy settings so that they can talk.

Early in our marriage I found it difficult to communicate at level three when I was sitting in our house. Rosemary would say, "Let's sit on the porch and talk tonight," to which I would answer, "Let's talk while we're hanging the wallpaper. That way we can get two things done at once."

It didn't work. We went into the bedroom to hang the wallpaper, thinking that we were also talking, but the priority was the wallpaper. In effect I was saying, "Just talking together isn't a good enough use of our time. Let's get something accomplished while we're talking."

We found it better to get out of the house. Since we were getting a baby-sitter anyway, why not go someplace? It was too expensive to eat a meal out most of the time, so we just got a cup of coffee, sat in the corner of a little restaurant, and talked for a couple hours. Getting out of the house helped us both stop thinking about all the things we should be doing around the house. It cleared our mental slates for that period of time.

Part of my job at Sheridan House is to help raise the funds for this charity. I learned early that the best place to get a businessman's full attention when telling him about our homes for children was certainly not in his office. If I could get him out to lunch I stood a better chance of communicating. Once again, if it's true for business, it's certainly true for home. And if it's worth doing in the business world, it's much more important to take this principle home.

Get out of the house if it will help. Find a little restaurant to sit and talk. It will cost a few extra dollars, but your marriage is certainly worth it.

As Donna and Billy had to realize, communication at level three doesn't just happen spontaneously. They had to set procedures. They had to decide if their marriage was worth the effort it took to set the procedures, or if they wanted to leave it to chance and spontaneity. Where my marriage is concerned, I don't want to leave anything to chance. All of us need to take our marriages more seriously than we do our businesses. Set those procedures in motion.

Summary

1. The first step to great marital communication is to recognize the need to set procedures.

2. The second step is to select the proper time of day and week for the best communication. Blend your calendars.

3. The third step is to see to it that there are no interruptions to your marital staff meeting.

4. The fourth step is to choose the best location for the staff meeting.

5. Decide that your marriage is worth the effort it will take to make these times of communication happen in your life.

Discussion Questions

1. When are you the most receptive to communication? When is your spouse the most receptive?

2. What are the hindrances in your relationship that make level-three communication difficult?

3. How do you respond when your spouse shares feelings with you? How does your spouse respond to you?

4. What are some steps you can take to get rid of the "invaders" of your communication?

5. Decide on a weekly time and place where you can count on uninterrupted time together.

Further Reading on This Topic

Communication: Key to Your Marriage, H. Norman Wright, Regal Books.

12

The Listening Ear

Vic has been a member of the board of directors of Sheridan House Family Ministries for years. One of his greatest strengths is his ability to raise funds. He is a great salesman, and people just like to follow his lead when it comes to making donations. One of the first times I asked him to come along with me on a visit to a potential donor's office turned out to be a tremendous learning experience for me.

We were escorted into the office of the CEO, who invited us to be seated. This potential donor's manner was very businesslike. He made me feel as if our time with him was going to be short. With this in mind I immediately launched into my talk on what Sheridan House was all about while Vic sat there with me. I could tell that I was losing the attention of the businessman as he began looking at the things on his desk. Obviously he wondered, "How did these guys get an appointment with me?"

After I rambled for about five minutes, Vic, the master salesman, cut into my pitch. He completely changed the subject and started talking about a photograph of the CEO and his family on their sailboat. They talked about the boat and boating in general for quite some time, and I was getting a little perturbed that Vic had gotten us off the track. The man was at least taking interest in the conversation at this point, however.

Finally this CEO looked Vic right in the eye and asked, "What can I do for you two?" To which Vic replied, "We've come to ask you to consider making a donation to Sheridan House." The man then asked, without looking over at me,

"How much are you looking for?" Vic responded by asking for an incredibly large number, and the man said, "That'll be fine. I can do that."

I was shocked. We were so close to being escorted out of his office, and then the meeting turned 180 degrees. It seemed obvious to me that what did it was the fact that Vic, the former pro-football player and top insurance salesman, did the asking.

When we walked out of the office, check in hand, I asked Vic, "What happened in there? It's a good thing you were along."

"It wasn't me, Bob," Vic responded, knowing that I thought the man must have known who he was. "I'm sure he had no idea who either one of us was before we walked into his office. We almost lost this opportunity for one reason. You never took time to listen."

What did he mean by that? The man never said anything to listen to. I was the first one to start talking. "Listen to what?" I asked.

"While you were talking," Vic explained, "I was 'listening' to everything that was going on." He went on to explain how he took in the man's environment, the things on the wall, the man's interest level in what we were talking to him about. It didn't take long for him to figure out that we were losing the man's interest. Then he finished our conversation with a statement that has proven to be one of the most valuable pieces of advice I've ever received. Vic said, "Decide ahead of time that you're going to listen with your eyes as well as your ears. Choose to take in everything so you can learn about the person you're trying to communicate with."

Choose to Listen

It sounds ridiculous to say that we have to choose to listen, doesn't it? Of course we listen to each other. How else would we be able to respond with answers? But maybe that's hearing rather than listening. Hearing we can do accidentally. We can hear without listening. You can hear a car pull up outside without really listening. Listening is something you choose to do. If you choose to listen to that car pulling up, you might be able to identify the car as belonging to a friend or family member. Listening goes deeper than hearing; it can also include perception.

A better example of choosing to listen rather than just hearing is the way we listen to our babies crying. I could be eating dinner at your house and your baby might be in the bedroom sleeping. All of a sudden the baby begins to cry. You listen to the crying and know that it's just a cry that indicates that the baby rolled over or is bored. It's not a very important call.

Later on that evening the baby might cry again. I look at you to see how you are going to respond and you recognize the cry as saying, "I'm wet. Could you change me?" or something that needs attention but is not urgent. Once again during that evening the baby cries and both parents shoot up and head for the bedroom. This time it's urgent.

I heard the three cries, but I didn't really listen to them. They all sounded the same to me. Not so for the parents. They chose to listen for what they could learn from each of the cries. They gathered information that allowed them to decide how to respond.

The Bad Habit

"You do it to me every time," Lorraine said to her husband, Phil. "You act as if what I have to say is of no value, but everybody else's opinion is important."

"Don't you think you might be exaggerating just a little?" Phil asked. "What do I do to make you think that I treat you any differently than anybody else?"

Lorraine went on to tell an all-too-familiar story that she felt typified the way they communicate. Two nights prior to this meeting in the counselor's office, Lorraine and Phil were out to dinner with another couple. Every time the other man's wife talked, Phil leaned across the table and made eye contact. He was actually making an effort to understand what the lady was saying. When the other man talked, Phil did the same thing. He made eye contact, nodding his head in agreement as the man conversed. Phil was making a conscious choice to listen.

When Lorraine talked, however, Phil looked off into space, looked at the menu, stared down at the table. He looked everywhere but at his wife. He looked interested when others talked, but he looked disinterested when his wife talked. In fact, he looked embarrassed, even cutting her off from time to time.

When Lorraine finished giving this illustration, proving how she felt he didn't listen to her, Phil said, "Oh, I think that's ridiculous! I don't do that!"

Then an amazing thing took place, right in the counselor's office. As the counselor would talk, Phil would sit up and look him in the eye. As Lorraine would talk, Phil would stare off into space as if he was bored. The counselor finally said, "Phil, you don't think that you break off eye contact when your wife talks, but you've been doing it right here in the office. It's a habit that you're not conscious of. When Lorraine talks, you act as if it's not important enough to concentrate on. You choose not to listen."

Many of us do that. We work at "listening" to other people, but we just "hear" when our spouses talk. We do other things while they are talking rather than decide to put everything aside and listen. It can become a destructive habit, and it must be broken.

The Central Nervous System

The job of the central nervous system is to maintain communication between the body and the brain. The central nervous system tells the brain that there is pain coming from somewhere that must be dealt with. It sounds an alarm. When there's a malfunction in the system and something isn't working properly, the "alarm" doesn't go off; it doesn't tell the person to do something about the problem.

Some years ago a professional athlete developed a bad infection on his heel. In the case of this athlete, there was a malfunction in the communications mechanism of his central nervous system. It didn't let him know how severe the problem was because it didn't really give off as much pain as it should have. He knew there was a problem taking place in the back of his heel but it wasn't communicating just how significant a problem it was. He let it go on without tending to it.

The infection progressed and became severe. Other complications developed, and this man actually died of blood poisoning—all because his central nervous system wasn't working properly.

The communication process has as its central nervous system the listening ear. It's more than an ear, it's the ears combined with the eyes and the heart. It's the whole system working together to assess what's going on around them. If there's a malfunction in the "listening ear" the whole communication process could shut down. This could culminate in a death of the system or the marriage.

Listen to Understand

Francis of Assisi once said, "Lord, let my quest be to understand rather than be understood." Sometimes when couples sit down to talk, one person makes demands while the other person can't even get a word in. We can issue edicts and never listen to try and understand what the other person is saying. Or we can stop, look, and listen. It's only when we stop, look, and listen that we are choosing to understand what our spouses are trying to say.

Listening is a developed art in this culture. People don't take the time to learn how to do it. Many pay professional listeners or counselors. One counselee said it well. He was sitting with his wife and the counselor. As his wife finished talking he turned to the counselor and said, "There. Now can you tell me what she means?" In other words, I don't want to take the time to learn how to listen to her. You do it for me and just give me the bottom line.

Other marriage partners keep looking for someone to listen. One day they find someone who actually counts them valuable enough to listen to them, but it's an acquaintance or someone at the office. Then they have an affair. It didn't start with the intention of having an affair. It developed out of the need to have someone listen. Perhaps just a few minutes at the office. Then a lunch together, listening to each other. Then the affair is launched.

There are questions to ask yourself.

- Have you already stopped listening?
- Do you have the habit of listening to everybody else but your spouse?
- Do you listen without interrupting?
- Do you allow time for long-term listening, or do all your discussions have to take place while driving to church because it's the only place you sit so close together?
- Do you listen with a clear mind?

Many people listen while formulating what they're going to say when it's their turn to talk. It's as if they're trying to win a battle rather than understand their loved one.

Listen to Learn

Decide to listen to learn. What is she saying here? Why is she saying it in that way? Why doesn't she just come right out and say what she means?

There might be several reasons. Perhaps she's afraid that I will become mad, or that I will turn her off if she doesn't hurry up and get it said. She might be afraid I'll act like it's stupid or that I'll turn this into a conflict. There are many reasons people talk the way they talk to us, especially our spouses.

We need to decide that we will listen so we can learn what our spouses are trying to tell us. What is she saying beneath the words? One way to find out is to ask questions that mirror what you heard. "From what you're saying it sounds like you think I . . ."

Your spouse is like that million-dollar donor. You need to decide to listen. Perhaps one of the elements most missing in our society today is the listener. People are lonely and look for ways just to have somebody listen to them. Some people even call radio talk shows, just to have someone listen to them. Those who feel as if no one is listening anymore often do drastic things to meet that need outside the marriage relationship.

Summary

1. The most significant component to the communication process is the decision to listen.

2. Listening is a conscious choice. Not listening can become a habit.

3. Many people don't even realize that they listen to everybody except their own family members.

4. Spouses who have no one listening to them can become very vulnerable to significant marital problems.

5. There's a big difference between hearing and listening. Hearing can be done by accident. Listening takes time and effort.

The Listening Habit Chart

How well do you listen? Take a moment to grade yourself on the continuum below and then grade your spouse. Then take time to discuss how you came to the decisions you did. The points go from 1 to 5, with 5 indicating the highest possible score for the particular question.

	LEAST SKILLED				MOST SKILLED
1. Am I a good listener when someone outside my family needs to talk to me?	1	2	3	4	5
2. Do I listen to my family when they need to talk to me?	1	2	3	4	5
3. Do I make eye contact while listening to my spouse?	1	2	3	4	5
4. Do I listen without interrupting?	1	2	3	4	5
5. Do I ridicule my spouse for having a different opinion?	1	2	3	4	5
6. When my spouse is talking to me do I look as if this is a very important conversation or do I look bored?	1	2	3	4	5
7. Do I allow time in my busy schedule for listening to my spouse?	1	2	3	4	5

Take time to discuss these questions. This is also a great tool to find out if your children and teenagers feel you are listening to them. Ask them to fill out the chart with you. You'll find out if they feel listened to.

13

But He Refuses to Talk to Me

*F*or several years I have had the privilege of co-hosting a radio talk show in south Florida. It's a broadcast where my co-host, Steve James, and I present a family topic and then, after a half-hour discussion, we open the phone lines for people to call in with questions. One night, when we were talking about marital communication, many calls came in with the same question, "But what do I do when my husband won't talk to me?"

There are many marriages where one spouse appears not to be interested in working on the communication process. I must say stereotypes do not fit here; I have found that almost as many wives as husbands are the deterrent to good communication in the home.

The basic question to be asked here is, "What can I do to help my spouse talk to me?" Before that question can be dealt with, however, there is a more basic question to look at. Why? Why is your spouse not interested in communication? Is there anything that has caused your spouse to shy away from in-depth communication?

Why?

Why is it that some people don't or are not able to communicate? There are probably some very basic reasons that some spouses don't communicate with their husband or wife. A few of these are discussed in the following paragraphs.

Never Saw It Done. Many people, especially in this generation, grew up in homes where they never saw their parents sit on the front porch and talk. Instead, their parents sat in front of the television and watched. Worse than that, they couldn't even compromise on what they wanted to watch so they went into separate rooms and watched different televisions.

Many of today's adults grew up in homes where there was no dinner hour, so they didn't have the opportunity to watch their parents interact. They never saw their parents deal with conflict. Never having the communication process role modeled, they don't know how to do it themselves. Nor do they think it's important.

"Hey," one man said, "all Margaret ever wants to do is talk. There's something wrong with her. My parents never just sat around and talked. They had too many things to do. What a waste of time." There are many people who don't know about the importance of communication because the marriage that they used as a model to work from never had any communication. There's an obvious parenting tip here. If we want to do our children a favor that will impact their future marriages, they need to see us dedicate time to the communication process.

Fearful of Exposure. Other spouses feel that they may be rejected if they express an opinion. Many children grow up in homes where they are not allowed to express opinions. In many of these homes, when a child or a newlywed does express a thought or opinion, the other spouse ignores it as if it isn't worthy of consideration. After a while it's not worth risking the rejection. It's just easier to avoid any form of deep communication with that particular person. Many times I have heard teenagers say, "It's just easier to tell my dad what he wants to hear rather than what I really think. That way I don't get laughed at."

Poor Self-Image. Often it's more than rejection. Some people have grown up in homes where they have had to endure verbal abuse. Years of being yelled at or being constantly ridiculed by a spouse could totally shut down any desire to communicate. "Any time I said what I thought," a woman said, "my husband responded with, 'You don't really believe that, do you? That's the dumbest thing I've ever heard.' I just got tired of listening to that, so I stopped trying to communicate. I found myself actually believing that I was dumb."

Nobody Is Listening. Many marriages go through cycles. Recently a couple came in for counseling because a disaster had taken place in their home. In the early years of their marriage the wife had done everything in her power to get her husband to talk to her. After years of trying and failing, she just gave up. Nobody was listening. She was just being tolerated. Now the shoe was on the other foot. He wanted to talk but she had long since given up. Many spouses stop talking because they know that their partner isn't really listening. They are tired of just being tolerated.

There are many other things that hamper the communication process. The key isn't finding the reason and then just sitting back and saying, "Well, that's why we aren't talking. Nothing we can do now!" The key is understanding that there is a problem and working on communicating with more sensitivity than you normally would need to use.

How?

"Every time we try to talk about things that are really on my mind," Debbie said in frustration, "Donald gets very angry." To which Donald responded, "I don't get angry at the fact that we're talking. What makes me mad is the way you talk down to me, as if I'm an idiot. You're constantly focusing on my downfalls."

So much was said in that exchange in the counselor's office. She was saying that she didn't know how to talk to him about the things that were affecting their marriage. Every time she did, he stormed out of the room. With that in mind, knowing that he was going to storm out anyway, she had learned to get as much out as she could, loud and clear, while she still had an audience.

He was saying he felt like she just spent that time ridiculing him. This communication thing was not a pleasurable experience for him because of the way it was handled. "I'm tired of getting slammed!"

This couple is very typical. Communication was very difficult for them, so she took advantage of any opportunity she had. If she had him alone for ten minutes she went "right for the throat." Donald no longer cared to talk at all. They needed a different approach.

Debbie finally asked a very crucial question. "How would you like me to bring up these topics?" Donald responded by saying that he felt inadequate as a husband every time she sat down to talk. Before she could protest Donald's statement, he held up his hand and said, "Let me finish!" Then he went on to say, "After we finish having these arguments, I realize that your statement to me, the one that caused the argument, wasn't as harsh as I initially took it to be. I had time to think about it. I guess I initially feel blindsided."

This was the beginning. He risked expressing the problem. In many marriages the noncommunicative spouse may not express these difficulties out loud. The spouse who is the communicator will have to analyze the situation and figure it out. This can be done by asking, "What am I doing to cause my spouse to become combative?" The answer may not be apparent but it's worth investigating.

Donald was saying that when he wasn't prepared for what Debbie was going to say, his natural reaction was to fight rather than talk. Over a period of time Debbie dealt with her husband by coming in fighting. A better way would be to give Donald some preparation time.

Here is a case in point. While I was sitting in my home writing this chapter, the phone rang. I answered the phone and listened to the ten-year-old son of a close friend ask me if I would pledge a penny a tree for each Christmas tree sold on the lot his Christian school had set up. My automatic response was to say, "Thanks for asking, Daniel, but we already helped

Sheridan House with their tree sale." After I hung up the phone I realized that he was really only asking for three or four dollars. He caught me off guard. My natural reaction was to put up a wall and politely say no. This, however, was something I could have easily said yes to. In fact, I would have liked to say yes. If I had been sent a note ahead of time it would have helped me think before I responded negatively.

That was the answer for Donald and Debbie. She analyzed the problem and decided to give her husband a little note about what she would like to talk with him about later that night. It gave him time. Time to analyze what he needed to do, as well as how he should respond.

Debbie needed to work on not attacking Donald in those letters, and that took time. But it did help them overcome Donald's desire to avoid talking at all costs.

Breaking the Cycle

When trying to analyze how to break the cycle of non-communication, it is important to look at how you can change your approach, like Debbie did. It's also important to go slowly. If a spouse has never experienced level-three communication, it's going to take time to get there. This can be very tough on the spouse who is the communicator. Tough it out anyway, for the sake of the spouse who is risking trying to do this new thing called "talk." Sure, you'd like to talk for an hour, but he only talked for fifteen minutes. Be grateful. That's progress.

Watch to see if he looks uncomfortable when you bring up sensitive topics. For now, in the early stages of risking communication, stay away from those uncomfortable topics. Be sure that you don't nag or criticize. If you do, the communication won't last very long.

Did this chapter give you the answers you were looking for to help you overcome your roadblocks? Perhaps not. The key is first to try to figure out why there is no desire on the part of your spouse to communicate. Then create a plan to slowly open the doors to communication in such a way that it will be plea-surable, rather than painful, for you and your spouse to spend time talking. It will take time, but it will be worth the effort.

Summary

1. There are reasons many people don't communicate with the people they love. Some spouses have endured very painful experiences when it comes to communication.

2. With many people communication needs to be handled with kid gloves. Some spouses need to develop a game plan that will make it easier to communicate.

3. It's important to proceed slowly when encouraging a spouse to open up.

Discussion Questions

1. Why do you think you and your spouse do not communicate?

2. How have you hindered the communication process in your marriage?

3. What things could you do to make your spouse feel more comfortable about communicating?

4. What steps are you going to take to develop better commu-nication in your marriage?

Part 4

The Exercise of
Conflicts

14

Conflict Aversion

I am told that men are ridiculous when it comes to going to the doctor. He feels a pain in his body and acts like it's not there. There must be something in the male gene that makes him act like he's invincible! If he goes to the doctor he will only find out there's something wrong, and he doesn't want to hear it. The sad part about this male quirk is the fact that if he goes to the doctor he will not only learn there's a problem, but he may find out how to take care of it. Instead, he'd rather walk through life acting like it's not there.

Pain in the body is a wonderful thing. It's an alarm that goes off telling the rest of the body there's a problem that must be dealt with. It's a very valuable tool. Years ago I was driving back from a speaking engagement. When we were about fifteen miles from home, the little red lights flashed on the dashboard. They were telling me that there was something seriously wrong with the engine. My daughter said, "Daddy, should we pull over?" To which I responded in a very all-knowing, macho manner, "No, honey, we'll be okay. We're just a little way from home."

We made it just a few more miles and then the engine died. I had to buy a whole new engine. All because I refused to respond to the signals. Whether it's a pain in the body or "idiot lights" on the dashboard, these are signals that shouldn't be ignored.

Conflict Is a Signal

Conflict in a marriage is similar to a pain in a body. Conflict is a signal that something is wrong or that something needs to be fixed. It's a signal that shouldn't be ignored or it will only get worse. Many people seem to think that conflict, if ignored, will go away. Not so! If you ignore it, it will only get worse.

Conflict Is Wonderful

Most people look at conflict in the wrong light. "I'm so depressed," one woman said when she called for counseling. "I didn't think we'd ever have a fight. My Aunt Alice was married for forty-two years and they never fought. We've been married five months and we seem to disagree on so many things. Maybe we're wrong for each other!"

Actually that sounds normal. The fact that her Aunt Alice was married for forty-two years and they never disagreed about anything means either Aunt Alice lied or that the husband was probably dead for forty-one of those years. Two people can't possibly live together and agree on everything. Conflict is that warning whistle that says, "Do something about this."

It's Not How Compatible You Are That Counts

Dr. George Levinger of the University of Massachusetts did research on the personality types that would be the most compatible in marriage. What two personality types would do the best job of blending and avoiding conflict? After much work he came to this conclusion: It's not how compatible you are that makes a great marriage; it's how you deal with the incompatibilities.

In other words, nobody is going to be compatible with another person (unless they're dating, of course). Once they're married, constant compatibility is impossible. We're simply different, and we're going to have different wants and desires. What counts is how we deal with the conflict.

What does conflict mean? That lady who called for counseling thought conflict meant she and her husband were not meant to be married. But if we operate under that premise, then we will do everything in our power to deny conflict because to admit there's a conflict is to say the marriage isn't good.

Conflict means many things, and the ultimate way to find out what the conflict is all about is to sit down and listen. There are some underlying reasons for conflict, however.

One is the fact that we're different. "She seems to like everything that I don't like. How can we possibly make it?" This frustration, vented by a newlywed husband, was only natural. Not until they got married and really got to know each other did they find out that they had so many differences.

This is normal. Not until two uniquely different individuals get married do some of these differences surface. These differences are due to gender and background. These differences are also fostered by personality types or temperaments that seem charming and interesting while dating but that take on a different light after marriage. One of the reasons for conflict, therefore, is the fact that we're different.

Not only are we different, but people also come into marriage with very unrealistic expectations. She may have expected her new husband to celebrate a holiday in a certain way or treat her in a certain way on her birthday. She can have all the expectations she wants, but expectations won't make those things happen. It's not fair either. He can't read her mind. He, too, may have expectations about things such as her housekeeping and cooking or the way she will respond to him in bed. Unmet expectations, what we fantasize that a marriage ought to be, can cause conflict.

It's a funny thing about expectations. People don't usually express them out loud. They usually just expect that that's the way things should be. As one lady put it, "If he can't figure it out, I certainly don't want to tell him. It will only ruin it. If I tell him the way I dream it should be, then it will become mechanical. He'll only do it because I told him about it."

Poor guy. He doesn't have a chance. He doesn't read the same novels she does, nor does he have the same expectations. He doesn't have any idea what she wants because she won't tell him. In this case, the problem just escalated until they ended up dealing with a tremendous conflict. Another reason for conflict, then, is our expectations.

Many times conflict arises over things that, on the surface, seem minuscule. But over a period of time, the fact that no one talks about it makes it a major area of conflict. He may be able to move on and forget about it. She may need to talk it out before she can forget it. There's a conflict because feelings are hurt even though the original problem no longer exists. "He should know what he's done to hurt my feelings. I'm tired of talking about it. We've been through this a thousand times," one wife said.

A young husband said, "That's ridiculous. How can she be hurt about the argument we had over her car? I went out and did everything she said needed to be done after we finished arguing about it. She won! I did it! How can she be upset?"

It's not the focal point of the argument that upset her as much as the way the argument took place. It's the things that were said and the way they were said. This husband felt guilty about the way he had exploded at his wife, so he thought he'd make up by doing things for her. That's very childish. He needed to go right to her and deal with what he had said. He needed to deal with the hurt feelings. Hurt feelings carry over to the next conflict.

Quite often many of the problems that couples have are really misunderstandings that are allowed to fester. Neither spouse can completely understand the other, and since we now go through life without sitting on the front porch talking, chances are we'll never know each other. That leads to situations where we just don't understand what's going on? That, in itself, leads to conflicts.

The man in the previous story thought he could make it up to his wife by doing things for her. He was project oriented. She was relationship oriented. He had damaged the relationship, and he didn't understand. These conflicts cannot be avoided by silence. Nor can they be glossed over by doing things for each other.

Nonverbal, Destructive Ways People Handle Conflict

It's easy to know that there's a problem or a conflict in the house. Some people only act like they don't see it coming. The logical way to deal with a conflict is to say, "I can see that there's something wrong. Let's set aside the rest of the evening, after the kids are in bed, to sit and I'll listen." That sounds too easy, doesn't it? Instead of doing this, however, people generally use nonverbal ways of handling their conflict.

The silent treatment is one of these. But the silent treatment usually isn't very silent. As a matter of fact, it can sometimes get quite loud. I remember when we were first married and I would tell Rosemary when I was coming home after racquetball. I would invariably be more than an hour late and not call. When I came in the door she would be very silent. Silent as far as any verbal input was concerned. I could, however, hear the kitchen cabinets being slammed. If I didn't take that as a cue to go in and talk to her, the slamming just got louder.

My first thought would be, *Here we go again. I hate giving in to this game. I'm not going in there!* That only made matters worse until I had to go talk for the sake of the cabinets!

The silent treatment doesn't accomplish anything. Often it only exaggerates the problem. She may be thinking one thing and be very cold and silent. He may take that as a sign that something far worse is going on. The silent treatment doesn't accomplish anything.

Another nonverbal reaction to conflict is a change in moods. We see this quite clearly in teenagers. Their whole life is so stricken with conflict that they become moody. It's the same reaction that some adults have when they don't know how to deal with the conflict. When a spouse becomes moody after a confrontation or marital conflict has taken place, it may be because he or she doesn't know how to respond. That nonverbal response needs to be approached with a verbal response. "I know you don't feel like talking right now. Could we just sit out on the porch and be together for a while?" After a while perhaps the person will feel comfortable enough to discuss the pain of the conflict.

Sometimes conflict can rise to such a state that anger takes over. Herein lies one of the most basic reasons it's better to deal with conflict rather than avoid it. Unresolved conflict can eventually become anger, and anger can manifest itself in some very irresponsible responses to life.

If a spouse refuses to talk about or deal with the conflict, further steps may need to be taken. A very significant step may mean going to see a third party, a counselor. At first this may only seem to further aggravate the situation because a spouse may not want a counselor's intervention. But it just may save the marriage.

A pastor's wife had taken all the anger she could handle. She told her husband that she was going for counseling, which only infuriated her husband. He didn't want anyone to know that they were having a problem. What he didn't realize was that his closest church members were able to hear his anger from the pulpit. It was affecting his preaching. She agreed not to go for counseling if he would be willing to sit and talk to her for two hours every week. That lasted for two weeks. Then he announced that it was a waste of his time and stormed out. She called the counselor the next day. Months later this pastor was willing to humble himself and follow his wife's lead. He came for counseling, and it probably saved his marriage and his ministry.

Ways People Handle Conflict

We all grow up in environments that teach us how to handle conflict when it comes our way. Many of these environments teach us very unconstructive ways to handle conflict. We may be willing to sit and talk about it, but we've developed a technique or two that get in the way of resolving the issue. Many times people have become so accustomed to handling conflict using their own personal unconstructive technique that they don't even know they are doing it. They think they're working at resolving the conflict when in reality they're still fighting or avoiding.

The following are some unconstructive techniques used to avoid dealing with the conflict. They may include a technique that you use and need to stop using. The discussion may, instead, bring to mind another technique that you sometimes fall back on when you don't feel comfortable dealing with a conflict.

The Hand Grenade Thrower. One example of this technique occurred when Jack was getting ready for his Thursday-night date with his wife, Barb. They were going to discuss their marriage, as they always do on Thursday nights, and he knew exactly what was going to come up. Last week they had talked about the fact that he needed to spend more time with the kids. He knew she was right about that, and he had pledged to do better. Unfortunately, since last week's discussion he had spent even less time with the kids. How was he going into this week's discussion?

"Barb, before we talk, I want you to know that I've just finished paying the bills, and we don't have enough left to pay the mortgage. I think we'll be okay, but it's really tight."

That was Bill's little way of throwing a grenade onto the porch where they were sitting. With something as big as losing the house "blowing up" on the porch, how important could spending time with the children this past week be? He thought he would derail his wife.

It didn't happen. Barb listened to the problem and waited for an appropriate time to discuss the children. But she

did discuss the children and their need for time with their father. The hand grenade did not blow her off the course that
really needed to be discussed. She just read her husband's
uncomfortableness and was sensitive in the way she handled it.

The Ambusher. The ambusher feels as if she will never get
a chance to sit and talk with her spouse, so she just takes little
shots at him whenever she can. This solves nothing. It may re-
lieve her of her anger by letting him know that she's upset, but
it makes him even more distant because he can't stand ducking
the shots. It makes the conflict far worse than the actual issue
that caused the conflict.

"When she would take those little shots at me," one husband said at a seminar after he heard this technique described,
"it would make me furious. In fact, it made me do those things
that she was talking about all the more. I know that's immature, but that's the way I responded to being ambushed!"

Obviously the ambush doesn't work! The nagging, the
constant correcting, and the negatives only further fuel the
conflict.

The Skunk. I'm embarrassed to admit this, but "the skunk"
is a technique that I have used. One day at 5:30 in the evening
I called home to say, "I'm on my way—be there in fifteen minutes." That's the arrangement we have so that my family can
know when to start dinner. The arrangement also includes a
stipulation that I will call again if anything holds me up.

This time, though, as I walked out into the parking lot at
Sheridan House, an older woman, whom I know, pulled up to
talk to me. There was no way to avoid her, since she pulled up
behind my car so I couldn't back out. I knew I should go back
in and call, because this lady always keeps me for thirty minutes. But I didn't call. Surely I could finish talking with her in
five minutes this time.

An hour later I pulled into the driveway at home. I didn't
call, and I knew by now the food would only be good for
hockey pucks! Since I was tired of giving excuses, I went in
smelling like a skunk.

As I walked in, I slammed my briefcase on the floor and growled about what a horrible day I'd had. The smell of rotten mood was so bad that nobody wanted to take me on and say, "How come you're late?" The skunk keeps people away.

Who wants to take on or confront a skunk? Who even wants to talk to a person who reeks of bad mood? The conflict never gets dealt with and eventually everyone around the skunk either gets in a bad mood or grows up trying to stay away from the skunk.

The Guerrilla Fighter. The guerrilla fighter is willing to sit down and discuss the conflict. The only problem is that the guerrilla fighter keeps changing the topic. Every time progress on the conflict is about to be made, the guerrilla fighter moves to another tree. This person changes the topic or the conflict to be talked about. "Yes, but what about when you . . ." Time is not spent working through any topic or conflict. This technique only keeps score. It doesn't solve anything. In fact, it tends to make the other spouse very frustrated.

The Lawyer. The lawyer uses a very sophisticated technique. He or she sits and listens to the other person. By all appearances the lawyer acts as if he is really thinking through the conflict being discussed. The other spouse feels, *Wow, this is great! We're actually talking about this*.

The lawyer only waits for his turn to talk. At that point he turns the tables and makes the problem the other person's fault. It's his job to place blame, and that blame will always be placed squarely on the other person's shoulders.

"Barb, I would spend more time with the children. The problem is you have this huge 'Honey Do' list that keeps me away from spending that time."

For a moment it makes sense to Barb. "Maybe it is my fault. Maybe I shouldn't be inviting the neighbors over for dinner. After all it only tends to interfere with Bill's time with the kids." Later on, however, when she finds him watching the ball game, not spending time with the kids, she thinks, *He's done it again. Instead of discussing it he's made me feel like it's all my fault*.

The lawyer turns the tables. That way blame rests on the other person and he doesn't have to do anything about it.

The Actress. The actor or actress becomes very emotional whenever conflict is discussed. It's hard to talk about difficulties if it only causes tears. Once again, this is a case of people being led to believe that any conflict at all in their marriage is cause for distress. They don't see the working out of a conflict as reason for joy and growth. Now that they are in a position to better understand each other as they talk about the conflict, they can grow in their marriage. If they can't grow, couples just stagnate at the wall of the conflict. They can't get past the wall because the actor or actress won't stop crying when they talk about it.

Tears can also be used as a tool of manipulation. *If he sees how this discussion upsets me so much,* she might think, *maybe he won't be so hard on me.*

The Comedian. There's nothing more annoying than people who are so uncomfortable talking about things that count, that they spit out little one-line jokes. They try to laugh their way through the problem. Usually their spouses have long since stopped laughing.

There are many things people do to avoid working on areas of conflict. They utilize these conflict-avoidance techniques either consciously or subconsciously. Some people have done it for so long that they no longer realize they're doing it.

Conflicts Are Good

If there's anything we would want to say in this chapter it is the *fact* that conflicts are good. Conflicts are not to be avoided. They are the warning lights. They tell us there's something that needs to be done. It doesn't mean that conflict should pit one spouse against the other. It's just the opposite. It means that the two spouses should sit down and work together to deal with the conflict.

Avoid statements like, "You do this . . ." or, "You never . . ." Just deal as a team with the conflict. Once again, it will mean compromise. Each spouse will have to give in to the contour of the other spouse's way of hearing things or talking about them—not fighting it.

Decide to talk about it. Decide to give the discussion as much time as it takes so that both of you can walk away from the discussion feeling like you better understand the other person. Most of all, decide not to win.

There's no winner here except the marriage. If one person wins the argument, then the marriage loses. Work as a team to listen to the idiot lights and discuss the warning signals. Help the marriage win.

We live in Florida, so it's almost mandatory that we have a pool in our postage-stamp-sized backyard. One year we bought a set of rubber rafts for the pool. The two rafts came packed neatly together in one box. After taking the rafts out of the box, where they fit perfectly, I decided to save the box to store them in after the summer. I put the box away and blew up the two rafts. Months later it was time to deflate the rafts and put them back in the box. Something had happened. I deflated one raft and, by itself, it would hardly fit back in the box, let alone the two rafts together. I worked and pushed and shoved and it seemed hopeless.

Once I got one raft in, there was just no room for the other one. Finally I realized that there were two things that needed to be done. First, I needed to make sure every ounce of air was out of each raft. Then I needed to roll up the rafts together, as if they were one thick raft. That way they could be forced into the box at the same time and the rafts wouldn't work against each other. They wouldn't push each other out of the way.

That's the way it is with conflict. First you have to get rid of all the "hot air." It just gets in the way. Then you have to decide to work on the problem together so neither one will end up pushing the other out of the way.

Summary

1. Conflict in marriage is a reality. Every marriage faces conflict.

2. Conflict is a warning light telling you there's an issue that should be talked about.

3. Don't avoid dealing with conflict.

4. Find ways to discuss it as a team rather than finding ways to find fault.

5. Check your technique. Look at the things you do that cause you to avoid the solutions to conflicts.

Discussion Questions

1. What are the things about which you seem to have regular conflict?

2. How are you handling these conflicts?

3. What conflict-avoidance techniques do you use? Which ones does your spouse use?

4. What are some constructive steps you can take to deal with these areas of conflict?

Further Reading on This Topic

Resolving Conflict in Your Marriage, Bob and Jan Horner, Family Ministry.

Husbands and Wives: A Guide to Solving Problems and Building Relationships, Victor Books.

Your Marriage Can Survive Mid-Life Crisis, Jim and Sally Conway, Thomas Nelson Publishers.

Everything You Need to Know to Stay Married and Like It, Bernard Wiese and Urban G. Steinmetz, Zondervan.

Dr. Dobson Answers Your Questions, James Dobson, Tyndale House.

21 Myths That Can Wreck Your Marriage, Barbara Russell Chesser, Word.

15

The Conflict of Finances

I don't know when it started happening. When we were first married we didn't have any money. When we didn't have anything and were almost starving, we never argued about it. We only dreamed of the day when we'd have a little financial breathing room. Now that we finally have some money, all we do is argue. That's ridiculous," one puzzled spouse said.

No, it's not ridiculous. It's a fact in many marriages. It is amazing to think that the blessing of having money can also become a great curse to the marriage. In one of his seminars I heard Larry Burkett, one of America's great financial advisers, say that battling over finances is the number one cause for divorce in our country today.

Money Is Like Sex

If you were asked the question, "How much money did your parents make?" or, "How did your parents make their financial decisions?" most people would be forced to respond with, "I don't know." We grew up in a generation where the handling of money was a very private matter. It was not an issue where parents called the children to the table to say, "Kids we're getting ready to make the monthly financial decisions and we need your input." Most children never knew what went on where money matters were concerned. Money was handled like sex; it was dealt with behind closed doors.

How, then, are we to know how to make money decisions when we grow up and get married? No one has ever taught us.

We have never had the opportunity to watch the give-and-take of two parents talking about money. On top of that, there were never so many financial decisions to make. Our parents just didn't have so many options. Nor did they have so many advertisers attractively displaying the options.

Money Represents Power

Money is a wonderful medium of exchange. It allows us the opportunity to get things and meet needs. It also represents power in our culture today. The people who control the purse strings are the ones who call the shots in industry, government, and even in communities. Not only have we not been taught about the many options out there for using this money, but we have been taught that it represents tremendous power.

"I felt like I constantly had to beg when it came time to buying anything," Betty said in exhaustion. "It's a constant battle over whether the things I want to buy are worthy or not. He makes me prove to him that we should have the item in question. Yet he goes out and spends as he pleases. If it's something for his bass boat, there's never any discussion. I feel more like an employee than a marriage partner."

Many spouses take advantage of the power money gives them by holding tightly to the purse strings. After a time of living with that power, they can begin to think nothing of abusing the family finances any way that pleases them. In a world where so many people seem to feel powerless, some grab for any power they can get their hands on. Handling the money can be just one of those "grabs" for power. Whether the one spouse spends the money in abusive ways or not, it can still lead to the destruction of the marriage relationship.

Money Can Own You

Money also can become a slave driver. Many couples become enticed by the advertisers and can be led to believe that they "deserve" the things they see. Whether or not they can afford these things is irrelevant. They can charge now and pay later.

Before they can get control of their spending and put on the brakes, they find themselves racing out of control toward financial disaster. It's tough to resist when there are new purchases being advertised every day. It's also difficult to resist when charge cards are so readily available. These temptations are almost impossible to resist when you have to make those decisions alone.

We all must choose whether we are going to spend our lives using money or spend our lives being used by the quest for more money. It will be our slave or our master. We can get into such debt that we must spend our lives doing everything possible to pay the bills.

We must also come to realize something that seems to have eluded our culture: There is nothing we can buy that will make us happy. Happiness is not a result of purchasing power.

Money Myths

There are some marital pitfalls to avoid where money is concerned. These are either misconceptions or immaturities that must be overcome when handling money.

Who Should Handle the Money?

Many of us have been taught a set way to handle the logistics of money decisions. Many in the Christian community still believe that it is the man's job to make all the money decisions, regardless of ability. That kind of thinking totally negates the "one flesh" concept.

The gender that writes the checks is not at issue here. What is at issue is who makes the decisions about what the money is to be spent on. There needs to be a "teamship" where financial decisions are concerned. Both parties should decide the spending priorities. Then the person who is more disciplined about handling the money could be the one to take care of the bills after the team has made the spending decisions.

It's My Money So I'll Spend It as I Wish!

In times past, when the man worked out of the home and the woman worked in the home, many men felt it was their right to spend the money as they wished. That certainly was not a teamship approach. Now we have a culture where many women work out of the home and bring to the family as much income as the male. This has caused some problems.

Many feel that since the handling of money is often used as power, they will not turn that power over to anyone else. Now we are in a time where many women feel it's their right to spend their money as they wish. In many marriages today, spouses divide up the bills, keep their own accounts, and hold total spending power over their income. It's never really income coming into the family or team, because the team never gets to work with the income. It's not coming in, it's being held as individual power.

Once again the teamship approach is necessary for the best handling and blend of the relationship. "I'll marry you, but I won't share my body with you." We would hope no one would say that to his or her spouse! As intimate as the sexual relationship is, a spouse would find no justification for holding back sexually. It is a basic part of the marital relationship to blend and share each other's body. Why, then, would some couples decide their money is more intimate than their bodies? It is for the good of the team that the money is handled together.

Why Should I Have to Account for Everything I Spend?

"I'd like to be able to share the handling of our money," a wife said. "In fact, I'd love it if he handled all our finances. It's exhausting to make these dollars stretch. But he hasn't any idea how to handle money. He'd just kept spending our money on junk until it was gone. Then we'd suffer until our next payday. I handle the money so we can eat!"

Many spouses are afraid to work as a team because they have been taken advantage of. "We'd make plans as to what we were saving for and what we were going to do with our money, and then the next thing I knew, the credit card bill would come in. He'd already spent the money without saying anything to me." Then this frustrated wife said something I will never forget. "I felt so betrayed when he would go out and impulse buy and spend all our money. I felt as if he had had an extramarital affair. Whatever it was he bought, he must have loved it more than his family, at least at the moment of the purchase."

It is the adolescent that feels he or she shouldn't have to account to anyone for what he spends his money on. The adult knows that life is one big accounting. If I'm part of a team, then I'm accountable to that team for how I hold up my end of the agreements.

Developing Financial Goals

The reason this chapter is preceded by chapters on communication is because communication is the key ingredient in winning the war over finances. Communication is a must. Any time two people of different genders and different temperaments try to decide how to handle money, staff meetings like those discussed earlier will be needed. But more than that, it will take a decision to fight the right war.

Many times, spouses fight each other using the checkbook. Consciously or subconsciously, they spend money in a way that they want to, so as to wound the other person. This shows they have autonomy. They'll spend money however they please. It's their "right"! There is a war, but your spouse is not the adversary.

Other couples go into the battle with only one fighter. One spouse may feel that dealing with the finances is too difficult or causes too many arguments. That person just sits back and lets the other have free rein. What that spouse is really doing is letting his or her spouse fight the war alone.

There is definitely a war waging. The war is a financial one. Whether it's a war on national debt, church debt, or family debt, if it's not fought properly it will lead to a downfall. God placed two brains in the marriage. It stands to reason that both should be used when fighting this war. Even when the finances are complicated and one partner may not understand all the ramifications, it's still important for both to make the spending decisions together.

Staff meetings where both spouses are able to sit and decide on the spending and saving is the way to deal with this financial battle. This is the time to establish or review the budget and decide whether it's providing the right boundary lines. Budgets are not very popular. In fact, they are so unpopular that our culture has created a way to avoid being hemmed in by a salary or budget. The budget buster is the credit card.

I grew up in a neighborhood where there were lots of kids my age. We'd get together after school and play touch football in the field by my house. The games almost always ended with massive arguments. The arguments would start over the boundaries or lack of boundaries. We didn't have any sidelines on this makeshift playing field, so to meet the need for sidelines, four guys would take off their shirts and place them at each corner of the field. The sideline was this imaginary line from shirt to shirt. That was fine when you were near one of the shirts. When you were in the middle, however, no one was ever really sure whether you were just out of bounds or just in bounds. The lack of observable boundaries meant that there was constant arguing.

When a couple wants to function as a team as they play this difficult game called finances, they desperately need some very observable boundaries. A boundary in financial terms is a budget.

I knew it, you're thinking. *Now we're going to be treated like inept children and placed on a budget.* No, that's not the case. In fact, it's only disciplined adults who can establish and live within a budget. It's Congress that has been shown to be the out-of-control adolescent, incapable of saying no to spending, unwilling to establish a budget that will keep us out of debt and trouble. If we're screaming at Congress to live within a budget, how much more necessary is it for families to operate within a budget?

A budget is mature, and it's good business. It also helps the other teammate make decisions. The boundaries are established, and the budget can't be broken unless both parties deem it necessary. That stops anybody from impulse spending.

There are many great books out today on establishing budgets. The back of this chapter lists a few. Work as a team; read one of these books together and set up a budget.

I know that doesn't sound like much fun. Budgets might seem very dry, with nothing left for fun. That's why I think it's important to budget in fun. In our home we use three tools to budget in fun.

Years ago I got tired of being the man who always said no. My daughter, Torrey, would ask, "Can we get a pizza tonight, Daddy?" She would walk away almost as soon as she had asked, because she knew the answer she was going to get from Mr. No.

We set up a glass bottle and put money into it the first and fifteenth of every month. The same amount of money would go into the bottle each time. This became the family entertainment money. When it was gone, it was gone—the well was dry until the next payday. Now when they ask for pizza or a milk shake on the way home from church, my response is, "I don't know. How much is in the bottle?" The burden of decision is on them. They have to learn to live within a budget. It also helps them plan ahead and begin, in a small way, to learn how to budget. They learn that if they want to go to the movies on the weekend, pizza is not possible tonight. We can't do it all financially, but many adults never learned that when they were children.

We do the same with our marital entertainment. We set aside a certain amount of money each month to do things as a couple. It's nice to know that the money is there so that we can go out to eat at a restaurant that is priced at the amount that we have. I don't care if you're a millionaire, it's important to set a budget and let other people bear the decision with you.

This is especially good training for the children. Regardless of the family's financial status, the children need to understand budgeting. The little glass jar will help them learn to make financial decisions. "How badly do we want that pizza, anyway? Badly enough to forgo something else this weekend?"

It's also important for each spouse to have what some might call mad money, money that they can use any way they want each week or each pay period. There's nothing more frustrating than to work in or out of the home, day in and day out, and not be able to spend a little money on something frivolous. Budget in a small amount of spending money for each, and then get out of the way and allow your spouse to use it as he or she pleases.

Dreams are important, too. Every couple should have financial dreams and goals. I am a person who sets goals and goes after them, even if I bruise everyone along the way. For many years I had financial goals, such as paying off the mortgage early, but I never talked about these goals with Rosemary. When she didn't know why I was so frugal, she just thought I was stingy.

One New Year's Eve, many years ago, we started discussing goals and got on the topic of financial goals. I told her, for the first time, that one of my goals was to pay off the mortgage early and I told her why. It was amazing how her attitude changed. She was excited to see I had this goal, but she was hurt that I hadn't shared it with her before then.

From that point on we decided to set aside time at the beginning of each year to establish goals for the coming year, financial as well as other goals. We would first review last year's financial goals and then set next year's. What bills did we want to pay off, how much did we want to pay down on the mortgage, how much did we want to save? We also developed a list of things that we wanted to buy in the coming year. We discussed how to prioritize these purchases. Did the need for a new lawnmower come before the need for wallpaper? That's when a very important ingredient came into play—the willingness to compromise.

Compromise

When establishing goals for finances, it is important to realize that God has put you together with a person who thinks very differently. He's put you two together for a reason. It's to help each of you to make wise decisions. The only way to take advantage of this different kind of thinking is to be willing to compromise. While making our list it became instantly apparent that my wife thought a new living-room chair should be higher on the list than a new gas grill.

We compromised, set the goals, and started at the top. The fourth item wouldn't be purchased until the first three were taken care of. If some unforeseen things took place, we would decide together to change the order on the financial goals list. Working as a team we understood where we were going financially, and we were less apt to make the other person angry or feel disenfranchised.

Working on finances together can be a blessing. Taking them on as a team will help you win the war. If not, financial difficulties will divide you and conquer your marriage. Remember the woman whose husband spent as he wished regardless of her input? She felt violated, as if he were having an extramarital affair with spending.

Summary

1. Money is like sex. Husbands and wives need to work on it together.

2. Money represents power in our society. Don't use it as a power over your spouse.

3. Have marital staff meetings or dates where you discuss your financial decisions.

4. Establish a budget so that you have boundaries that each of you understands.

5. Share your financial dreams and goals.

Discussion Questions

1. What financial decisions do you make as a team? What are the financial areas that you need to do a better job of working together on?

2. What can you do to help keep your family within your established budget?

3. What are your financial goals? What are your spouse's financial goals?

4. When are you going to meet to discuss your budget and your goals?

Further Resources That Can Help You

The Complete Financial Guide for Young Couples, Larry Burkett, Victor Books.

Master Your Money, Ron Blue, Thomas Nelson Publishers.

16

Lovemaking from a Woman's Perspective

Bob would say this chapter is about sex. I prefer to say this is the chapter that talks about making love. That, in and of itself, shows how differently the genders approach the whole topic of sex in marriage. To the woman, it's the physical culmination of a deeper relationship. To the male, it's a physical response that stands completely alone from the relationship.

"That explains it," one lady said in the counseling room. "I never could understand how we could fight all the way home from a party and Ed would still want to make love when we went to bed. It was the furthest thing from my mind, but it was the only thing on his mind, even when we weren't getting along."

There Are Two Myths

For the past few decades, movies and other forms of entertainment have led us to believe that men and women both respond to the sexual aspect of a marriage in the same way, that they are both "turned on" by the same things. The fact that men are visually stimulated has led some men to act as if woman are the same. Hence the development of pornographic shows for women, including male strip joints.

In reality, women are much more complex and don't respond in the same ways men do. It's a myth that causes conflicts between many husbands and wives. He doesn't understand why she was not turned on by the visual stimuli of a movie.

The second myth is the Victorian thought process about wives and sex. The Victorian myth is that woman don't really enjoy sex, at least not physically. According to this myth, sex is just something to be endured. Nothing could be further from the truth. Yet many women in our society are in situations where they must endure the sexual relationship in their marriages because of a lack of understanding.

Dr. Marie Robinson, in her book *The Art of Sexual Surrender*, has indicated that millions of women in America today suffer from Hypoesthetic Syndrome, or frigidity. It is her premise that this dilemma is taking place predominantly due to couples' lack of education on the subject.

It is important to remove both these myths from the marriage bedroom. Women do approach the sexual relationship differently from the men, and they are able to enjoy this relationship. They just enjoy it in a different way.

Experience Rather Than Physical Release

A wife sees her sexuality as a physical expression of the larger, more encompassing relationship she has with her husband. The whole relationship, which means spending time together talking or just being together, can lead to sexual love on a particular night.

This was best summed up by a wife who was trying to explain her need for time together before they made love. "That's foreplay for me," she said to her husband with tears rolling down her face. "The whole evening is foreplay for me. Talking, touching, sitting together on the couch, or going for a walk. All these things are what I need to be able to feel like making love. I've begun to see that you men don't need these things. You can ignore me all night and still want to make love when we go to bed. Foreplay for you is when we touch each other in bed. It takes about two minutes. Foreplay for me takes much longer. It takes a relationship."

In her agony she was trying to explain that she felt used when he didn't want to meet her needs for relationship. He thought she was just like him, "It's bedtime, so let's make love."

It has been well said that wives give sex for love. But there's another side to that adage. Husbands must give love for sex. When both are trying to meet the other's needs, then both are more able to find fulfillment in the sexual aspect of their relationship.

She's looking for an emotional, as well as a physical, experience. She also deeply needs to feel cherished. That's why when he uses street talk to describe sex together, it makes her feel cheap and, once again, taken advantage of. She doesn't feel like an equal partner in the experience.

Her Needs

It is extremely important that a husband work at understanding his wife's lovemaking needs. She has more prerequisites than he does. She's looking for oneness; he's looking for instant gratification.

Because women are much more intricate in their needs, it's often true that many women don't know what their needs are. "Our sexual relationship was great for the first year of our marriage," a husband said, "but then I could see that she was losing interest. Was it something I did?" It was probably something that young man didn't do. He didn't talk to his wife about their sexual relationship. When she didn't have the opportunity to talk about her likes and dislikes, she didn't have the opportunity to better understand her needs. Thus she didn't have a chance to learn about herself, sexually speaking.

The Atmosphere. A woman has a much greater need for creating an ambiance where lovemaking is concerned. She's more sophisticated about the situation. Surroundings are more important. She needs more privacy. That's why she may be concerned that the kids are still awake or that there's company in the next room. Where a man may be just as happy in the back seat, his wife might be more excited about a bed and breakfast inn. She wants to feel as if she's worth the effort.

In the Bible, Solomon knew these important ingredients. He very systematically prepared a special bedchamber for his new wife. The intricacies are described in Song of Solomon. He wanted her to feel special, as well as loved.

The condition of the master bedroom will help. It's funny that we live in a culture where the master bedroom is the last place that we take care of. It's the last place we decorate. It can be the drop-off point for toys or the mail. It can even be where we dump all the laundry as it waits to be folded. We take very poor care of this room that's supposed to encourage intimacy.

Cleanliness. "I wish he would understand how much it turns me off when he comes after me and he is still filthy from a day of work!" She experiences lovemaking using all her senses. A woman needs to feel as if she is worthy of his getting cleaned up for the occasion.

Several Levels of Love. She needs to feel loved in several different ways. There's a friendship side to love. As has already been said, she needs to spend time with her husband as a friend, not in competition with the television. She doesn't want to think that the only time he wants to be with her is when he wants to make love. She needs to feel liked as a person, as well as desired.

She needs the sensitive side of love. He needs to see her need for help with the various areas of her life. "It surprised Bill to hear that it turns me on when he helps me with the evening activities," Janet said at a seminar. "I really appreciate it when he pitches in and helps with the kids and the dishes. It shows me he cares about me as a person not just a body."

Most wives have the desire for romance. Romance is defined in many different ways by different people. When we did a survey, one woman at a seminar said the most romantic thing her husband ever did was compose and sing a song for her. Another woman said it was the way he looked her in the eye when they talked. For me, it's when Bob gets dressed up and we go out to dinner at a nice restaurant. "Romantic" means different things to different women. The key for each husband is to find out what his wife perceives to be a romantic gesture.

For a woman, lovemaking is an event. When possible, a whole evening should be set aside to talk, touch, and love each other. Again, Solomon was wise as he discussed this (Song of Solomon 3, 4). He and his bride looked forward to and prepared for their evening together with expectation.

Still another ingredient to totally loving a wife is to recognize her need for affection. Affection is the verbal and physical expression of love with no sexual connotations.

Affection is not physical foreplay. Affection is a hug with no strings attached. When we were first married, how many times did I say to Bob, "Couldn't you just hug me rather than grab me?" This is an expression of love that indicates to a wife that she is loved even if they don't make love that night. She needs to feel that her company is valuable to him just for who she is rather than for what she will do.

When these four expressions of love are met—friendship, sensitivity, romance, and affection—it opens the door for the next expression of love, physical love.

It is obvious that God intended for a woman to experience tremendous physical pleasure in marital lovemaking. He provided a specific point of pleasure at creation. We know of no other reason for that little organ, about a centimeter in size, above the opening to a woman's vagina. It is called the clitoris, and it's there for sexual arousal.

In physical foreplay, the clitoris and the woman's breasts are two very sensitive areas of arousal for her. There's no way for a man to learn the best way to arouse her while petting or touching these areas, without her instruction. This whole idea is a beautiful gift from God. He has placed us in a situation where a man and a wife will have to learn to talk to each other while making love if they want to bring each other to sexual fulfillment.

For a man not to be willing to talk and take instruction means that he will end up meeting just his own sexual needs and never finding out the nature of his wife's needs. She will not be interested in a sexual relationship for very long under those circumstances.

For a woman not to be willing to help her husband understand how she wants to be touched means she will miss out on the opportunity of sexual fulfillment or improving their sexual relationship. "But I don't know myself!" one woman said in the counseling room. "How can I help him know how I like to be touched if I don't even know?" "That's when it's time to practice moving your husband's hand into different locations if you feel funny talking to him while making love," was the counselor's reply. "Show him."

She Has a Sex Drive, Too

A woman has a sex drive, too, but it's different than a man's. Where a man experiences each sexual experience as separate from the last, a woman generally does not. Each of her lovemaking experiences builds on the last one. If the last time she made love with her husband was an exciting experience, she will look forward to the next time with anticipation. If the last time she made love with her husband was a painful or otherwise unsatisfying experience, her enthusiasm will be dampened.

Her sex drive is not as regulated as his. While his is tied to a physiological build-up of semen, hers is wrapped around events and relationship. Fatigue will also play a much greater part in her ability to respond sexually. Because her sexuality is so much a part of her total existence, if a woman has had an exhausting day, her sexual battery will be affected. Not so for a man. It's as if a woman has one battery that fuels her whole being. A man, on the other hand, seems to have a battery that fuels his being, and then he has a separate little battery that is ready for sex regardless of how tired his body may be. That battery doesn't seem to run down.

Sex Is a Learning Experience

There's no way a man can possibly understand a woman's sexuality unless he has help. It's mandatory that husbands and wives talk to each other. It's also very important that they each adopt a specific sexual attitude. If each spouse accepts the goal of making the other person happy, then each will be able to assess the other's needs. They will each work hard at discovering what makes the other person happy. In the long run, with two attitudes like that at work, this couple will be very fulfilled sexually.

Summary

1. It's a myth that men and women both respond to sex in the same way. They are very different.

2. It's also a myth that women don't really enjoy sex as much as men do. They're just different.

3. Women see lovemaking as part of their relationship with their husbands, rather than standing alone from the relationship.

4. Most women want to be loved at several levels. They want friendship love, sensitivity, romance, affection, and physical love.

5. Women have a sex drive that is related to previous sexual experiences with their husbands.

6. Lovemaking is more intricate for a woman. It's not as biological and requires more learning. The husband and wife must help each other understand their wants.

Discussion Questions

1. Ask your wife if she feels she needs the various aspects of love which include friendship, sensitivity, affection, romance, and physical love.

2. Do you feel you meet the needs that she has? Does she? How could you do better?

3. As a couple, discuss what you think are the things that could be hindering you, as a wife, from being totally fulfilled in your sexual relationship.

4. What steps can both of you take to make these adjustments?

Further Reading on This Topic

Hold On to Romance, H. Norman Wright, Regal Books.
Love for a Lifetime. James Dobson, Multnomah Press.

17

Sex from a Man's Perspective

Bill was what could be called a typical male in today's culture. He grew up in the Midwest, in the home of a businessman. His father never sat him down and talked to him about sex. He meant to, but that ominous fishing trip where he would tell his son about the "birds and bees," never took place. Bill's sister got the information she needed because she was a girl. When her parents knew it was about time for her to start her menstrual period, they knew they had no choice. They had to talk to her. Plus they wanted their daughter to understand what boys were interested in.

Bill, on the other hand, got no information at all from his parents. The things he learned about sex came from his friends, first from comments of conquests in the locker room and then from fraternity brothers in college. All they ever talked about was conquering girls and sexual prowess. No one ever talked to him about girls and their needs. Sex was never talked about by his parents in the beautiful way God planned for it to be, so it was a very difficult topic for him to ask questions about. "I mean, what kind of *man* has to ask questions about sex?" he would say to himself.

Then he got married. To add to their difficulties, Bill and his fiancée, Denise, were sexually active before they got married. That meant that they didn't talk much when they were dating. Instead, they searched for places to have sex.

Things changed after the marriage, however. Denise seemed to be less interested in making love. Now that they were married it was no longer a taboo, so it was no longer "fun" to sneak. She didn't really understand that she had robbed herself by violating God's plan for purity before marriage. Now it was routine and something that seemed like she was obligated to do. It hadn't changed at all for Bill, and he couldn't understand what was happening to Denise. She had become very distant and didn't like even being touched by Bill.

Bill had not grown beyond the biology of sex in marriage. He desperately needed information, but wasn't able to get it. What became obvious was that Denise, though she seemed to enjoy sex in the same way she did before they were married, was now very different.

Bill knew he needed help, but he didn't know how to go about getting it. Denise knew he was searching for answers, even though he didn't come out and ask. She, too, wondered why they were so different in their approaches to lovemaking. She had places she could go for information, however.

Denise began reading articles in magazines about husbands and wives. Some of the things she learned about men fit her husband; they also disappointed her. She didn't realize that sex in marriage to a man was so unemotional, so physical.

The Biology Is Very Strong

It's a fact that men are very responsive to the biological sex drive. It's actually a choice that they have to make. Either they control their drive, or their drive controls them. This drive builds in pressure to the point where the pressure wants to be released. This release is called ejaculation.

It sounds very mechanical and unromantic. In and of itself it *is* very mechanical, if the husband decides to take care of only his own needs. If that's all he does, however, he finds very quickly that his wife is increasingly less interested in making love. Her needs aren't being met, so the experience becomes less pleasurable.

There's a Plan Here

God, in His infinite wisdom, has created men and women to be different for a reason. What appears at first to be a conflicting part of the marriage relationship is, in reality, a powerful blending force. If husbands and wives both responded to sex in the same way there would never need to be any communication. If women responded from a biological perspective, as do men, husbands and wives would never have to learn about each other's needs. In fact, they'd never even have to talk to each other. They would just convene every other day and take care of their needs.

God obviously planned for the sexual relationship to be a powerful force that would draw a husband and wife into a deeper relationship. To truly enjoy each other sexually, they would have to get to "know" each other. Hence the Bible, when referring to sex between husband and wife, sometimes uses the term "know," as in "knew each other." Husbands and wives must quest after knowing each other's needs.

Visual Stimuli

Biology is only one part of the formula for the male sex drive. Yes, it is very regulated by the biological buildup of semen. Usually the semen almost "screams" to be ejaculated every forty-eight hours or so, depending on the man. But there's more than the biology.

Men are stimulated or triggered by sight. They respond to visual stimuli. That's why many men want the bedroom light left on. Denise made the comment, "I have learned that I'm in trouble if I undress and get ready for bed in front of Bill. He can have given me no indication that he was interested in making love as we head to bed, and then I get undressed while he's watching and his switch is turned on."

Advertisers understand that very powerful force in a male. If they want the male's attention, they include an attractive female in the ad or on the billboard.

"It makes me mad," one wife said. "It makes me mad to think that the sight of another woman can make my husband think about sex. I think it's an insult to a wife!"

She's right with her statement but wrong with her approach. She's right that it's an insult and her husband should try to understand. On the one hand he wants his wife to feel cherished, and yet he spends time looking at other women walking by. "What harm does it do if I don't touch?" a very adolescent forty-year-old commented. A great deal of harm. It hurts your wife and it hurts your thought life.

A wife finds it difficult to respond if she feels as if she's competing with other women that her husband looks at. Imagine how a man would feel if, around her neck, his wife wore a picture of a man and on the back of the picture it said, "A great lover and makes $200,000 a year." "Why do you wear that around your neck, Dear?" the husband might ask. "Because he's the man I look up to. Not to marry, but I just like to imagine what it would be like to spend time with him and have him spend money on me."

If the husband was normal he would feel very jealous. (The men reading this chapter with their wives right now will say to her, "Not me, Honey. I wouldn't be jealous!" It's not macho to be jealous of competition. Baloney!) A man should understand that he's creating tremendous conflict within his wife when he looks at other women. If she feels her husband enjoys looking at other women, it makes it difficult when he wants her to take her clothes off with him. He's actually causing a sexual conflict within his marriage. That's why many women find it difficult to be totally free sexually when their husbands want to watch sexually explicit videos before they make love. The visual images may stimulate him, but they shut her down. "It breaks my heart," a wife said in the counseling room, "that I'm not enough to make him sexually excited."

It is an insult to a wife for her husband to use or look at other female bodies to get sexually excited. This aspect of the visual orientation of the male may be very disconcerting to a wife, but it cannot be ignored. That needs to be stated again. The fact that a man is visually oriented cannot be overlooked by a wife. She needs to understand her husband and do what she can to help him "rejoice in the wife of [his] youth" (Prov. 5:18 NIV). There aren't a lot of lingerie stores for men; at least I hope there aren't. Yet there are many for woman. Wives should learn to take advantage of the opportunity to use them.

Dressing to Please Other Men

In general, women should acknowledge that they understand the visualness of the male. In so acknowledging this fact, they should take it upon themselves to dress in such a way as to not encourage other men to look at their bodies. "Oh, that's archaic," I can hear some women say. "If I want to dress in a certain way, I'll do it. If a man has a problem with that, it's his problem, not mine."

Here again we can easily see that we are an immature society. Many don't care to act in a manner that will help those around them. A friend of mine recently discovered that his daughter has juvenile diabetes. His family has decided that, for a while at least, they will all go on the same diet that she must go on. "Is that really necessary?" I asked him. "No, we don't all have to drop the things from our diet that Lauri has to, but we decided that we wanted to help her. If she didn't see us with some of those foods, then it would be less of a temptation for her. We didn't want to get in the way of her dealing with this aspect of her life."

That's the answer for all of us, isn't it? Men need to understand that they are visual and that their visual nature needs to be dealt with. Men need to indicate to their wives that they won't insult their wives. They won't make their own thought lives more difficult to deal with by giving in to the visual temptations. Women need to understand that their husbands are made the way they are, not because they're operating at the animal level, but because that's the way they're made. It's something that must be accepted and dealt with. In connection with that, women need to understand that the way they dress is very important.

The Conscience

Men are visually stimulated and very biological, but men also have a conscience. They have the strong desire for a sexual relationship, and yet they have a conscience. Many may say that the conscience is a thing of the past in today's society, but that hasn't proven to be true in my twenty years of counseling experience.

After an affair, many men are plagued by tremendous guilt. Perhaps the more they violate their vows, the more they ignore their ability to feel a conscience. The conscience is there, however.

God decided to give man, who lives with this dilemma of biology vs. conscience, a gift. It was the gift of guilt-free lovemaking. No doubt it's part of the binding of husband and wife. In marriage, a man and a woman have the opportunity to love each other and meet each other's needs without feelings of guilt. That certainly makes a man love his wife even more. Man can choose a marriage relationship rather than wake up the morning after a "one-night stand" and regret what he has done or compromised for the sake of an ejaculation. God has given this gift of a clear conscience via the wedding vow.

Frustration and Sex

"What's this stuff I always hear about men becoming sexually frustrated?" a woman asked her friend over coffee. "What does it mean for him to be frustrated?" Her friend responded with, "Frustration is real. I can tell when we haven't made love for a while. Many times the barometer is my husband's attitude. It may even be that he's been too busy and falls asleep every night in his chair; sometimes it's not even my fault that we don't make love. But then he gets testy. He argues with me over things that we shouldn't be arguing about. I've learned that one of the factors that may be plaguing him is the fact that we haven't made love for a while."

There's much wisdom to what this experienced wife was telling her friend. Somehow there's a link between the sexual or biological state and the emotional state. A man can become very frustrated with life or his marriage and not even know why. It may not even be his wife's fault that they haven't made love, as was the case with this wife, but it may still leave him very frustrated.

It could also have an impact on his thought life. Since his sexuality is biologically regulated, it will be more at the forefront of his thoughts if he has not experienced a satisfying sexual relationship at home. With his sexuality at the forefront he will have a more difficult time dealing with the visual stimuli he sees daily. This is not an excuse for sin. It can certainly be resisted no matter what the temptations might be. A man who has made Christ the core of his life can overcome all temptation: "Greater is He that is in you, than he that is in the world" (1 John 4:4 KJV). Nevertheless, it will add to the battle.

It Takes Work

There's obviously much work to be done. There are still other questions to be answered about the sexual relationship in marriage, and the next chapter is dedicated to these additional questions. The key is a willingness to learn. The greatest approach spouses can take in their sexual relationship is to decide to meet the other's needs rather than to take from the spouse to meet their own needs. The decision a spouse makes to sacrifice his or her own happiness in order to make the spouse's happiness a priority will have a tremendous impact.

It's more than a coincidence that God gave couples an opportunity to learn this concept of sacrificing for the sake of another person's happiness via the act of sex. Babies are born as a result of the act of making love. When a baby enters a couple's life they learn that nothing is too great a sacrifice for the needs of the baby. They read books to learn about the needs of the baby. They sacrifice sleep, resources, and everything they have for the baby. The baby's needs become a focal point.

This just may be God's way of teaching us how to sacrifice for the happiness of another. How great would a couple's sexual blend be if they both decided to learn about each other's needs and then make them a priority!

Bill's Dilemma

In the beginning of this chapter we talked about Bill's lack of knowledge. Not only did Bill enter marriage without being taught about women (as do most men), but he didn't feel he had any place to go for information.

"Denise's magazines all have columns on marriage," Bill said in frustration. "My sports and news magazines don't have a whole lot to offer on the marriage relationship! I feel like I'm left out without any way of getting help." No sooner was this out of his mouth when he saw the look on his wife's face. He decided he'd say it before Denise said it. "I know, Honey, for years you've been ripping out helpful articles and putting them on my bedside table to read. I've found them very helpful . . . as iced-tea coasters! I guess I haven't really been trying to find help, until now."

Well said. There is help available. It comes in three forms. First, there are always articles that can be found in women's magazines that will be very helpful for both spouses to read. It's a matter of a husband being willing to learn and receive information. It's definitely to his advantage to learn.

There are also many books that are great manuals on sex in marriage. Writers such as Dr. Ed Wheat and Tim and Bev LaHaye offer excellent books that will help a couple grow in their understanding of each other. These books and articles are best used when a couple sets aside the time to read out loud to each other. That way the material can be discussed and learned together.

When a couple is not able to overcome the sexual difficulties it is time to see a trained, Christian counselor who has an understanding of this area. This third source of information can be tremendously helpful by providing objective input.

There is help. It's just a matter of taking advantage of it. For years Bill and Denise just sat back and said to themselves, *Well, we're just too different to be sexually compatible*. Then, with help, they discovered that their differences were not only normal, they were a great asset. As Bill and Denise grew together in understanding, they not only became happier sexually, they really began to know each other in a new dimension. Now they were focusing on each other's needs.

Summary

1. A woman is oriented around relationship and a man is driven by his biology.

2. Most men are without a clue as to how different their wives are from them. Worse yet, many don't read the information available to help them understand the differences.

3. A man is also very visual when it comes to his sexuality. His sight is a key to his desire for sex.

4. A man's thought life is a difficult area for him to control, especially if he and his wife are not relating sexually.

5. It would seem that God, in His infinite wisdom, has made men and woman different in their approaches to lovemaking so as to force them to have to communicate and thus "know" each other better.

6. Husbands and wives must decide to teach each other or they will miss out on what God planned for them in their sexual relationship.

Discussion Questions

1. Describe the differences in your responses and your spouse's responses to sex.

2. Describe to your spouse the areas you think could be improved in your sexual relationship.

3. What are some steps that can be taken to make these improvements?

4. What are things that you could do to improve the way you respond to your spouse's sexual needs?

18

Sexual Issues Spouses Sometimes Argue About

*I*t's so much easier to talk about making love when it has to do with other couples. It's harder to discuss it when I have to sit and talk about it with my spouse. When it's about me, personally, then the real issues and inadequacies surface. With that in mind, we have compiled some of the questions that we are asked at marriage seminars. These are included with the hope that they will help spouses do a better job of communicating about sex, an issue that is often difficult for husbands and wives to talk to each other about. As a matter of fact, we have found that invariably, one of the spouses in each marriage finds it difficult to talk about their love life.

For some reason it's hard for us to talk to each other about our sex life, but we both know we want to improve it. How do we begin talking?

The fact that most of us grew up in homes where sex was not discussed means that sex seems to be a taboo topic. In past generations, parents had very obvious examples and illustrations of procreation. They lived in agrarian settings where the animals supplied the opening opportunities for discussions about sex. Parents also took the time then to go into the deeper, more beautiful aspects of sex beyond procreation.

For the past two generations this has not been done. Hence, we have spouses who never grew up talking or learning about sex from their parents, so they feel extremely awkward talking with their spouses about sex. Many men can talk at their spouses, telling their wives what they want out of sex. Few can sit and take lessons from their wives to learn about their needs.

The way to begin discussions on sex is to use the help of an expert. At the end of this chapter is a list of books about sex in marriage. Purchase one of these books and read it out loud to each other. The best way to begin talking about this very significant topic is to allow the book to present the various issues and then discuss the topics and ideas presented.

It can't be stressed enough that the best way to utilize this material is to read it out loud together. Read a chapter, or half a chapter. Then put the book down and talk. "Does this apply to us?" "Is that the way I treat you?" "Does that describe your needs?" Use the book to stimulate the conversation.

My spouse doesn't respond sexually in the same way you discussed in the previous chapters. Is something wrong?

These chapters are written in generalizations. They describe the majority of people, but people are different. In some marriages it is the husband who is better able to talk about feelings. This is also true for romance. Sometimes it's the husband who has a greater desire for romance than the wife.

Frequency of need for sexual activity can also vary due to a number of circumstances. In the previous chapter we talked about the fact that a man's sex drive can be very regulated. With some men it's every forty-eight hours. This can be true of a man for many years, and then he can enter a time when he can go a month at a time with no apparent interest.

Depression, exhaustion, or job-related pressures can temporarily depress his desire for sex. He can become consumed with pressures from the outside world that overwhelm him and tend to make him uninterested in sex. Most marriages experience this "sexual valley" at least once.

Current situations in life can have an impact on the sexual relationship of a husband and wife. Previous situations, such as childhood, can also have a tremendous impact. Men or women who were sexually abused as children or young people can later experience tremendous sexual difficulties when married.

One young husband, a new Christian, made a tragic comment about this area. "We made a lot of mistakes before we were married. We weren't yet Christians, so we didn't understand the damage that can be done by premarital sex. My fiancée, who was sexually abused as a teenager by a member of her family, thought that she expressed love by giving me sex. For her, sex before marriage was easier than lovemaking after marriage. She gave it of her own free will before marriage. After marriage, she felt it was once again being demanded by me, and this seemed to remind her of the abusive situation she had been in. It was only after we became Christians and sought counseling that she was free from our past mistakes and her previous abusive experiences."

Are there sexual activities that a husband and wife shouldn't do? We argue a lot about things that my husband wants to do and I don't feel comfortable with.

The fact that making love is so personal and intimate means that we get very little counsel from wise people as to what is appropriate and what isn't. Many couples argue over issues such as oral sex or various sexual positions. These are issues that can't be legislated as to what is right and what is wrong. Right and wrong needs to be answered by each individual couple.

There are things that are unacceptable in married love. Sex should be a beautiful expression between a husband and wife—and them only. It should be an expression of each other's love for the other person. Anything that makes one spouse feel less prized, or is demeaning, is unacceptable.

A husband must decide that, rather than making demands, he will make concessions to his lust for new and yet uncharted territory in his bedroom. A husband might say, "If you love me, prove it by doing this." He needs to show his wife he cherishes her by saying, "I love you and it's obvious that you really don't want to do this, so I won't ask you to. This is a token of my love."

The movie industry has made sex look like something one takes from another. That perspective is all wrong. Making love between a husband and wife is something that you give to each other. Give freely toward a wife's happiness and a husband's excitement, but experience sex in a way that will not be demeaning or painful to your spouse. Experimentation is exciting as long as each partner is willing, rather than one partner demanding.

Is it wrong to look at sexually arousing movies or magazines before making love?

Many couples today have put themselves in a position that they believe they can only be aroused by looking at the bodies or actions of models in sexually explicit situations. This is not only contrary to God's plan for the intimacy of a husband and wife learning to rejoice in each other's sexuality, but it is also addictive. Using an individual other than one's spouse for arousal is a tremendous slap in the face for one's spouse. It tears at the self-esteem of the spouse. It is as if a husband says, "No matter what you do or how you look in a nightgown, you will not be able to excite me." It should not be surprising, then, that the man's spouse will find it difficult to even want to respond in a sexual way. She can't compete with the pictures.

Sexually explicit pictures and movies also have a polluting impact on a man's thought life. He fantasizes about women that he's not married to. Why does it surprise us that God's ways make sense? God is not a kill-joy when He commands a monogamous marital relationship. He just understands what is best and right for the creatures He has created. Using visual aids for arousal is not only wrong, it is tremendously detrimental to the marriage and the individual.

We were sexually involved before we got married. Now that we have been married for several years, I feel as if my wife is angry with me about the fact that she wasn't a virgin on our wedding night. Is this normal?

Most women carry a dream of giving themselves totally to their husbands. That virginity is her dowry on her wedding night. There are many women today who are angry with the man, even if it's her husband who robbed her of the dream. There are also many women who are angry and sexually unfulfilled in their marriages and don't know why. For a great many of them this is the underlying problem.

Even though she consented to be sexually involved prior to the wedding, this doesn't lessen the disappointment she lives with. She's disappointed in her own personal lack of discipline as well as disappointed in the fact that, by pressuring her, her husband-to-be didn't help her fulfill this dream.

This is very difficult for the male to understand. His sexual expression is predominantly physical. Hers is an expression of herself and her response to the magnitude of the relationship. Hers is an ongoing expression of love, rather than an explosion that is quickly over. He shouldn't try to identify with it; he should instead try to help her through it.

It is the wise husband who will realize this disappointment or anger. Nothing can change the tragedy of the circumstance, but a husband can sincerely ask for forgiveness for the part he played. This could do much to start the mending.

Why doesn't my wife want the bedroom light left on when we make love?

This is a difficulty for many woman. Our society has made them feel physically inadequate. She is not as visually stimulated, so the light means little to her sexual arousal. In fact, it makes her feel self-conscious.

Today's woman is constantly being bombarded by catalogs showing her how she should look but doesn't. The women in the magazines, as well as the beauty queens on television, are paraded as a reminder to her that she is inadequate. Add to that the fact that many husbands stare or even comment about other woman as they walk by or appear on television. These gestures on the part of her husband only tend to demean the way she feels about herself physically. Why, then, should she try to compete by turning on the light and taking off her clothes?

This is a very harsh world for the physically aware female. She is forced to take constant personal inventory of her physical appearance. It is a wise husband who lets his wife know how beautiful she is. Unfortunately, most husbands seem to take delight in criticizing their wife's weight or other aspects of her appearance. These are the same husbands who later wonder why she won't leave the light on.

We hold a great portion of each other's self-esteem in our hands. A husband who loves his wife enough to understand the beauty battle she's in will counteract the critical world his wife lives in. Let her know she's beautiful. Let her know she is loved for who she is as a person rather than for her personal appearance. She doesn't need to hear from her husband about her flaws. She's painfully aware of them already.

I don't know how it has happened but somehow our lovemaking has gotten to be very boring and routine. What can we do?

Unfortunately, the world responds to that question by saying, "Find a new partner." Nothing could be further from the truth. It's not a new partner that is needed, it's a new approach.

Every marriage goes through this crisis. Some couples do nothing about it and their sex life shuts down altogether. Others choose to do something about it.

When a couple's sex life becomes boring it's probably because each spouse has started to take the other for granted. Choose to change. In Ephesians 5, husbands are told to "love your wives" (v.25 KJV). That means they must cherish their wives. The man needs to think of how she would like to be romanced and not just reach over and kiss her after spending a night watching the ball game. Cherish her needs and wants.

This same passage also says, "The wife must respect her husband"(v.33). The woman needs to respect his need to feel like somebody in her eyes. Has she ever approached or seduced him, or does he always have to suggest it? Create an affair within your own marriage.

It's also significant to get out of a sexual routine. "Well, it's Saturday night and we always make love on Saturday night, right after our Saturday-night television program is finished." That's incredibly unexciting and obligatory! No wonder people are so easily blindsided by extramarital affairs.

Get creative about when to make love and where. Several years ago, a lady we're proud to call a friend wrote a book called *Total Woman*. It's humorous that while many talk-show hosts ridiculed Marabel Morgan's approach to marital creativity, everyone else wanted help with their need for a creative marriage. That year Marabel became the world's number one best-selling author of a nonfiction book.

We all need to decide to beat the "blahs" by getting creative. Even if the other spouse doesn't seem to be interested in getting out of the rut, it's important to try to pull or even entice him out any way possible.

For many people an answer to the blahs has been taking a second honeymoon each year. They get out of the environment where boring habits have been developed and go away as a couple. A romantic weekend or a week at a bed-and-breakfast inn or mountain cabin has an amazing way of helping couples spend time falling romantically in love again.

"Oh, but we couldn't afford that. It would cost too much!" It would cost a lot less and be a lot more fun than counseling fees or the compulsive purchases people make as a result of boredom. Set a date for a second honeymoon that will be long enough and far enough away for you to leave your routine for a while and just be together. Don't go with another couple.

Is there any way I can help my kids with this difficult area of sex in marriage?

There are several ways we can ease the burden on the next generation. First, we can give them the information that we didn't get. Talk to your children about their sexuality. Don't expect your church or school to do it. It's not their job.

Children need to be taught at an early age. Get a book such as *The Wonderful Way Babies Are Made* by Larry Christiansen and read it regularly with your children. Make this a topic that is always open for discussion. By doing this, you will be doing your future in-laws a tremendous service. If children grow up in homes where sexuality is easily discussed, they will be able to discuss it with their spouses. As difficult as this discussion with our children sounds, it just may save their marriages.

Parents also need to show their children some of the nuances of romance. Children need to see their parents get dressed up to go out to dinner as a couple. When Rosemary and I go on trips to speak, many times our daughter has been in the room while my wife is packing. She has observed Rosemary pack some very sexy negligees.

When I was a little boy, every Christmas season my dad would take my brother and me into New York to shop. Two things were inevitable on this trip. One was that we would have lunch at a restaurant that delivered your plate on a Lionel train. The toy train would stop right in front of where you were sitting and you took your plate off the train. It was great!

The second tradition was that we would go into Macy's department store and Dad would buy my mom a sexy negligee. We couldn't believe he was doing this, let alone doing it with his two boys along. It was agony to be a little boy with your dad in the negligee section of a store, and he seemed to take so long making his selection! Nothing much was said, so we just figured that the store must be near the restaurant.

It was only years later that I found out how far the two were from each other. It was only after I had been married for years that I realized that it wasn't really the special Lionel train that he wanted us to see. He was training his boys for a romantic marriage. Help your children out.

Further Reading on This Topic

Sexual Happiness in Marriage, Herbert J. Miles, Zondervan Books.

The Act of Marriage, Tim LaHaye, Bantam.

Intended for Pleasure, Ed and Gaye Wheat, Fleming H. Revell Co.

The Intimate Marriage, R. C. Sproul, Tyndale House.

Intimate Marriage, Charles M. Sell, Multnomah.

Solomon on Sex, Joseph Dillow, Thomas Nelson Publishers.

Celebration in the Bedroom, Charlie and Martha Shedd, Word.

The Power of Sexual Surrender, Marie N. Robinson, M.D., Signet Books.

Sex Facts for the Family, Clifford and Joyce Penner, Word.

Part 5

Get Aggressive

19

Goal Setting

Picture the opening of a corporation's annual meeting. All the stockholders are there, anxiously awaiting a word from the board of directors. A representative of the board steps up to the podium and says, "Next year we have no real goals or direction. We're just going to keep moving on."

If that ever happened, everyone would be rushing to a phone to tell his stockbroker to sell. That company wouldn't be around very long without any goals. Goals are extremely important.

Every institution knows the significance of goals. Goals supply the direction. A goal is a motivator and a reason to go through the drudgery to get to a certain destination. I'm willing to go through this drudgery because I know where I'm headed. When I get to my goal it will be worth all this effort.

If we find it important to set goals in industry, in churches, and in every other viable organization, why is it that most married couples don't have any family goals?

The answer to that question is once again cultural. In years past, husbands and wives worked together on the same project. If they were on a farm or owned the general store, they both worked to build the business. They had a goal, spoken or unspoken, to work together and sacrifice for the sake of attaining the goal of building the business.

Today's married couple does very little together. If they don't sit down and plot a course for their marriage, chances are they will never reach any goals. It's a pretty basic principle. If you don't try to get to a certain place, or goal, there's a good chance you won't.

When couples don't have common goals they get derailed very easily. They purchase things they don't really need, and they get involved in relationships that are detrimental to their marriage.

Setting Goals

Once a year the Barneses have a longstanding date to sit down and review last year's goals before we set the next year's goals. For us that date is New Year's Eve. For other couples New Year's Eve is a very unrealistic time to go out to eat with a folder marked "Annual Goals" under their arm. Set a date that suits you better if you need to. But you do need to!

We set goals in several areas of our marriage each year. Then, since July 1st is midway through the year and our wedding anniversary, we review our goals then. It's not important what dates you set to work on the goals; it's just important that you do it.

Setting the goals is only the beginning. If you don't establish a way of reaching your goals, then it's really only a dream. A goal is a direction you decide to go in. A dream is something you just wish would happen, but you don't do anything about it. Dreams fade away if they don't become tangible goals.

Establish a Plan

Now for the work. A goal needs a plan of action if it is to be attained. Most couples just go through life working, but they don't have any goal that they're striving for. They are going through life just working hard. It takes a combination of a goal and an action plan to get you to that goal.

It's drudgery to work when there's no goal at the end of the tunnel. That's when couples become disenchanted with the relationship. Yet what they don't realize is that it's not really the relationship that they are unhappy about. It's the fact that they are working hard every day and they don't feel like they're getting anywhere.

"I began to feel as if we were losing ground in so many areas," a young man said in the counselor's office. He had been married for eight years, and they had been arguing constantly for the past year. "Financially we're in a deep hole; we seemed to argue about everything we did with our money. On top of that our kids are out of control . . ." He went on to give a list of the things that were going wrong. Then he said something that made the counselor stop him. "Now my wife can't stand to be with me. I had so many dreams for us and . . ." "Wait a minute, Jack," the counselor interrupted. "You said you had so many dreams for your family. Have you ever shared those dreams with your wife?"

No, he hadn't. That's typical. Many spouses have dreams, yet they never take the time to share them with each other. So they stay dreams rather than becoming goals because the couple never works together to set up an action plan. In fact, they often work against each other's dreams without realizing it.

A couple must set a time to meet and then share their goals with each other. After talking through the goals, each spouse must be willing to compromise as they prioritize them on paper. At that point these goals are no longer the goals of an individual. They are now the goals of the family. With that in mind it is important that one spouse does not ram his or her own personal goals down the throat of the other spouse. Bullying to get your way will only destroy the whole process.

The next step is the action plan. How will we get there? What do we need to do each week or each pay period to accomplish this goal that we both deem worthy?

Finally, when will we evaluate our progress? Set a time to look at or talk about how you're doing in the pursuit of you goals. Some goals, such as paying extra money down on a mortgage payment, are self-evaluating. You can rejoice each month as you write the check. Other goals that aren't quite as obvious can slip away if they aren't scheduled for evaluation.

Each person reading this chapter may decide to set goals in different areas. The following are areas that we have decided we want to work on each year. As the corporate head would say, these are the products we want to turn out this next year.

Spiritual Goals

I believe that each of us was placed on this planet for a purpose. I believe I was created as part of a plan, and I don't want to miss my part in that plan. The only way to get closer to the mark is to grow closer to the One who created both me and the plan.

Each year we set goals for ourselves, evaluating whether our personal growth is closer to what Christ would have us be. I don't want to be a religious person as the world defines religious, going to church just for the sake of going to church. I want to be active in my church, grow closer to Christ, learn more about Him, and help my church carry out its mission.

Spiritual growth is my responsibility, however. My church can't do it for me. By the end of the next year what do I want to have done as far as spiritual growth is concerned? Perhaps, for those who haven't already done it, establishing a consistent daily time of reading the Bible and/or a devotional book is the first spiritual goal to look at. What will you do personally to assure that you will not remain static in your spiritual development? Actually, you never stay the same. If you stop working toward a goal, you slide backward.

What about spiritual growth and your marriage? If your spouse is a partner who believes as you do, a worthy goal would be to decide to pray together each night. If your spouse does not believe as you do, then decide to find a time to pray for him or her each night.

Rare is the couple who are at the same place of spiritual growth all the time. Most couples vary when it comes to who is the person who is the most spiritually "tuned in" at any particular time.

Is Your Spouse Totally Uninterested?

Many who are reading this book might be married to a person who is totally uninterested in spiritual growth, or anything spiritual, for that matter. The goal for that reader would be to find a way to encourage the other spouse toward spiritual things.

"I've done everything in my power to get my husband to want a spiritual dimension in his life," a wife said to her pastor. "He's just not interested in knowing more about Christ. He even throws out the tracts I put out for him to read."

There are two key phrases in her statement. One is the phrase "to get my husband to." Nobody can get, trap, or badger another person into wanting to step into a relationship with Christ. That's the job of the Holy Spirit. Many believing spouses actually push their nonbelieving spouses further away. Many wives talk about the church and the men at church hoping to make their husbands interested in meeting the people there. This actually does just the opposite. A husband can become very insecure, even jealous, when hearing about how wonderful the men at church are. He might even take it upon himself to find the flaws in these men, even the ones with whom he may interact in public or business. Be careful not to chase a nonbelieving spouse away.

The second phrase that this wife used was "throws out the tracts." Bible tracts are wonderful and have led many to Christ. If, however, they haven't worked with your spouse, another approach is necessary. For me, personally, as a young man on a college campus, it was the lifestyle of a Christian young lady (Rosemary) that brought me to the point where I wanted to know more about Jesus Christ. Many people are skeptical about Christians because in some cases there is an obvious inconsistency between what they say and how they live. A worthy goal would be to live a life that would be so Christ-like that it would draw a spouse toward the One who directs that life. Living a life of joy in difficult circumstances will have an impact.

What About the Children and Spiritual Goals?

The spiritual development of the children is a very important part of this goal-setting operation. How will you help them grow spiritually this next year? One way to start is to set a goal of leading the children in a family time of Bible reading or devotions.

Marriage Goals

What about goals for your marriage? Do you want to be in the same place in your relationship in the years to come as you are now? Even to maintain that you'll have to work. In what areas of your marriage would you like to grow?

Sexual Understanding

Most couples would like to work harder at understanding each other sexually. That's certainly a worthy goal. So purchase the books talked about in previous chapters. Set a time to read them out loud to each other and then ask questions so that you can reach a goal together.

Marriage as a Priority

All couples will want to work on keeping their marriage as a priority. A wife might place her family as a priority over her marriage. She doesn't mean to or realize she does, but her husband feels that she does. A husband might place his work or softball as a priority over his marriage. Whatever it is that makes the other spouse feel he or she is playing second fiddle needs to be dealt with. State the competitor (in-laws, job, etc.), and then develop a plan to deal with it.

Whatever it is, set the goal and then set the time to evaluate this particular goal every week. Be kind to each other or this will become a very touchy area. Handle the conflict properly. There may be other areas to set goals for, such as the joint care of the house or more time together, that a couple would want to set as a marriage relationship goal.

Financial Goals

As has already been discussed, finances are a major area of conflict in a marriage. An additional difficulty is the fact that most couples don't have any financial goals. And if they do have financial goals, they don't have the same ones. Set aside a time to itemize the financial things that need to be accomplished during the year.

We always have some dream goals on our list. This is either an item that is placed last on the list and will be purchased after all other items on the list are taken care of or it's an item that we will put some money away for, knowing that it will be purchased in the years to come.

Years ago we had a goal of a new house. We knew that goal could not be reached in one or even five years, so we set it as a goal. For seven or eight years we set aside a specific amount of money each month for our new-house fund. At the same time we worked at paying off the mortgage on the house we owned. We wanted to pay it off earlier than the mortgage due date. Because we were paying down extra on a mortgage, we were able to move much earlier than anticipated. It was made possible by the fact that we had a goal and stuck with it.

It's also important to include fun ways to spend money. Yes, this is also a financial goal. The goals need to include fun purchases and second honeymoons. These will ease the drudgery of saving for the future. Most couples don't realize how much money they spend on a day-to-day basis. They spend it because it's in their pockets, and they think that it's theirs to spend rather than to use in pursuit of a goal.

Parenting Goals

Couples who are parents will want to set goals for their children. These aren't goals for the children to shoot for. These are goals that the couple wants to pursue as the parents of the child.

What are the skills that my children will need before leaving home? How can I make those learning opportunities available to them? My children will need to understand who they are spiritually; I'll need to teach them. My children will need to know how to handle money; I'll need to give them an allowance so they can practice spending and giving. Children don't automatically want to tithe their money to the church. It needs to be taught.

All parents have pet areas they want to teach their children. Think through what these areas are. Get the resources or books to help you learn how to do it. Then put these things on the calendar to do. And, of course, don't forget to evaluate how you're doing in these areas at the weekly parental staff meetings.

Staff Meetings

Staff meetings to talk about and evaluate the process are very important. "It used to make me so mad," Jaynie said. "Bill and I would set the goals and then he'd go on and spend any way he wanted—just as if we had never talked. It wasn't until we started the weekly times of getting together where we could talk about why this was done or that wasn't done that we made any progress. Then we understood that we were heading in the same direction as long as we stayed with our goals. The weekly meetings saved us."

Recently, I heard a speaker use the following illustration. Picture yourself on a plane and the pilot comes on the public address system. "Ladies and gentlemen, we have some good news and some bad news. First the good news. We're now cruising at an altitude of thirty-five thousand feet at a speed of six hundred miles per hour. We're making great headway. The bad news is that the compass and radio are not working so we don't know where we're going."

That's the story in many marriages. They're going full speed ahead, but they really don't know where they're going. As a couple they have no goals. So guess what: They won't reach any goals together.

Summary

1. Set a time to talk about setting goals for yourselves as a couple.

2. Decide what areas you need goals in (spiritual goals, financial goals, marital goals, parenting goals, etc.).

3. Together, prioritize your goals.

4. Set a time to evaluate how you're doing and how you're staying on track as you head toward your goal.

Discussion Questions

1. What are your goals as a couple? Consider your spiritual goals, financial goals, relationship goals, and parenting goals.

2. Which of your goals creates the most conflict? Why? How can you compromise?

3. How and when can you evaluate your progress together as far as reaching your joint goals are concerned?

Further Reading on This Topic

Beloved Unbeliever, Jo Berry, Zondervan Publishers.
Creating a Successful Christian Marriage, Cleveland McDonald, Baker Book House.

20

Your Spouse's Self-Esteem

I can't possibly meet all her needs," Jim said in total exasperation. "They're never ending. She just expects too much out of me, more of me than I'm able to give!" This husband was stating a fact. No one person could ever meet all the needs of another person. However, there must be some needs that we are able to meet in the life of the person we're married to.

In Genesis 2 God saw that it wasn't good for a man to be alone. He was incomplete. So God put a man and a woman together so that they could help complete each other. The puzzle parts could fit together. It's almost as if God allowed Adam to see the animals all paired up and then realize, "Hey, I'm incomplete!" The fact that man and woman were, and still are, different helps them complete each other's empty portions.

"But why is it that she needs me to constantly reaffirm my love for her?" this husband went on to ask. "Why is she so weak and insecure?"

It's not at all because she is made to be weaker or more insecure. It is because she has a greater understanding of the responsibilities involved in maintaining a mature relationship. This man's wife was looking for a relationship in which they would each communicate how they felt about things and how they felt about each other. She did not want just a once-and-for-all, "Of course I love you! How could you not know that? I told you that ten years ago! Did you forget?"

Just because this husband may not understand the different needs of his wife doesn't mean that she is inferior. Actually, it probably indicates that she is more sophisticated in the area of relationship needs. The fact remains that she has lived with and anticipated some emotional togetherness that she hasn't received. This has left her emotionally empty.

Meeting Each Other's Self-Esteem Needs

No, we cannot meet another person's self-esteem needs entirely. But we can and must meet the self-esteem needs that the marriage was meant to meet. A spouse plays a part in his or her partner's completeness. And a spouse plays a very significant part in his or her partner's perception of self and the value of that self. The marriage relationship is very significant as far as emotional well-being of a person is concerned.

If you doubt that, take a look around you. One man said, "You know, I thought that was ridiculous until my vacation this past summer. The contrast I saw when visiting my two sisters was absolutely incredible. I didn't think a husband's attitude toward his wife could have an impact on her self-esteem until we met my older sister and her family on vacation. I hadn't seen my sister in a long time, and I had to work at hiding the shock when I first laid eyes on her. She looked horrible and couldn't even pick her head up and look me in the eye. This was a girl who had been on the homecoming court in high school and was one of those "most likely to succeed" types. Now she cowered like a whipped dog. I wondered what had happened until I heard her husband talk to her. He was very cold and demeaning. He had broken her spirit and her confidence.

"To tell you the truth," this young man went on, "I didn't even want to continue on our vacation and visit my younger sister. I just wanted to go home, but I'm glad I didn't. My younger sister, who grew up in the shadow of our older sister's successes, used to be very shy and insecure. Pulling into her driveway and seeing how happy she was as she ran out to our car actually brought me to tears. She, too, was a different person than I remembered. She was happy and confident, and it was easy to see why. She and her husband, Ed, had a great relationship. It was easy for all to see how much they loved each other. It sure showed me the impact I can have on my wife."

This whole vacation had an impact on the way this man treated his wife and family. He saw that the interaction that takes place between husband and wife will help to create an environment for the enhancement or destruction of his spouse's self-esteem.

Self-Esteem of a Woman

In the book *Dr. Dobson Answers Your Questions*, James Dobson talks about the number one problem that women reported having—low self-esteem. It may be one of the leading causes of depression. And it's little wonder when you look at the battle that today's women must fight.

The media spend much of their time trying to define who today's woman is supposed to be. In this beauty- and youth-oriented culture, she's to stay eternally beautiful and slender, regardless of how recently she's had a baby or how many babies she's had. The modern woman must be a super mom, be career oriented, and maintain an exciting marriage, all at the same time.

As the media have attempted to push the modern woman in these directions, she has found herself more unfulfilled than ever before. The woman is the relationship expert of our species, yet the modern approach to womanhood makes her so busy that there's no time for relationships. She's looking for relationship, most especially the intimacy of a marriage relationship, yet today's society has robbed all the relationship time from the marriage. Consequently, she's unhappy.

Relationship is an area for which the man she married is totally unprepared. She yearns for marriage as a mature, ongoing relationship. He has no idea what that means. He knew how to have a relationship when they were dating, but now they're married and he has no idea what to do.

Her Self-Esteem Is Out of His Comfort Zone

"I know that she wants me to work harder at our marriage, but I have no idea where to begin. It's just easier to stay at work longer and buy her a nicer home." This is a typical, often-heard response to the dilemma. Instead, what is needed is a husband who is willing to learn about his wife's self-esteem needs and then step out of his own personal comfort zone and work at these needs.

"Do I really have to do that?" one husband, married nine years, asked. "Do I really have to do something that is so hard for me to learn to do?"

The answer to that is found in the Bible, in Ephesians. "Husbands, love your wives, just as Christ loved the church and gave himself up for her" (Eph. 5:25 NIV). Husbands here are told that they need to love their wives the same way or to the same degree that Christ loved the church. How far did Christ go for His church, His bride? The question at hand is, did He step out of His comfort zone?

The minimal word that could be used to describe Christ's love for His bride, the church, is sacrifice. He sacrificed everything He had, His position at the right hand of God (temporarily), His safety, and even His life. I'd say that was out of His comfort zone. Christ came to meet a need and it cost Him His life. He's telling husbands to sacrifice for the sake of their wives.

The wife has a desire to know that she personally is cherished and that the marriage relationship is cherished. She wants to know that it is not for her performance, how good she is in bed, how good she looks or cleans house, but for what she means personally to her husband that she is cherished. A person who is cherished is encouraged and continually reminded how much she means to her husband.

The steps for a husband to take are twofold. The steps he needs to take will answer the questions, What does my wife need to feel adored? Am I willing to step out of my comfort zone to meet those needs?

Many husbands wonder why their wives have turned to other areas in order to fulfill their self-esteem needs. "My wife doesn't even want to take vacations with me anymore. I guess I've waited too long to act like a husband. Now she's invested her whole life in the kids and there's no room for me. I created this monster, and now I don't know how to turn it around."

When a person continually gives to a relationship and receives nothing in return, he or she eventually looks elsewhere. Some wives look to parenting to meet their self-esteem needs, some to careers, and yet others turn to other relationships. It may be a step out of a husband's comfort zone, but it's worth the sacrifice.

A Man's Self-Esteem Needs

Men grow up learning a very different mode of operation than do woman. In the past, boys learned about delayed gratification while helping their dads on the farm. It took a long time to see a response to the planting, and there was much to be learned from the waiting period. As was discussed in the first chapters, today's man hasn't been trained on the farm. He's been trained with a short-term gratification, Little League mentality; the game lasts two hours. He now has a short-term goal orientation for life. Our culture has changed radically in the past century, and this has impacted the thought process of the male.

Today's man has been misinformed by his upbringing. He has been taught that life is one performance after another. People are either competitors or they don't really matter. His self-esteem is enhanced by working his way to the top. When he gets there and has all the toys that go with being at the top, then and only then will he truly find happiness. The trouble is, only one in a thousand actually gets to the top, and the rest of the men find disenchantment or dissatisfaction. Little do they know the ones who make it to the top are just as unhappy. "Oh, yeah?" I can hear a man reading this saying. "Well, I'd sure like to try their dissatisfaction!"

The male desperately needs to be complete in the marriage relationship, but he has been taught that if he needs anybody other than himself, he must be weak. It's hard for him to let down his guard and admit that he needs someone else. It's even more difficult if he is constantly battling his wife on issues at home. When he battles his wife and feels as if she doesn't respect him, it makes him even more insecure, which usually makes him less mature in the way he handles the relationship. His answer will be to spend more time away from home or shut down as a husband all together.

It has been said, "Behind every successful man is a great woman cheering him on." Cheering him on because he's worthy of her cheering? Probably not. In the same book that tells husbands to love or cherish their wives, it says. "the wife must respect her husband" (Eph. 5:33 NIV). Why? Because her husband is respectable? No, it doesn't say, "and to those of you wives who have respectable husbands, respect them."

Respect is a posture or response to another person that one chooses to take. I don't always agree with the one who has been voted into office as president of the United States, but I still respect him. I may not have even voted for him, but I respect his position. A wife has already cast the vote for her husband at the altar.

The fact that husbands are performance oriented means they respond or are repelled by the way their wives handle their husbands' leadership. When the book of Ephesians talks to wives about submission, it is not telling wives to be doormats. Quite the contrary. It is encouraging a wife to give a husband all the advice and input she has. It is telling a couple to blend and learn to respect each other's opinions (Husbands, sacrifice for your wives as Christ did for the church). But when it comes to a decision where a husband and wife cannot come to common ground, one person has to be held accountable for the final decision. A couple can't work together as a team without some final consensus. When God indicates that a woman is to submit, He is saying give all the input you have and then if your husband still disagrees let go of the argument. God will hold the husband responsible for the final decision.

Performance Orientation

Wives can have a great impact on their husbands' self-esteem if they understand that men are performance oriented. One way that this performance orientation is expressed is through the husband's provision for his family. A man has a tremendous need to feel that he can materially provide for his family. Wives can do much for their husbands if they are satisfied with the lifestyle they live. Wives who continually express desires for more things such as new cars and bigger houses can cause a man to feel as if he is not able to provide as he should.

A wife can also do much for her husband's self-esteem if she uses her mouth wisely. I have seen just as many husbands as wives who have been scarred by the degrading words of a spouse. These are scars that last for a long time.

A wife loves to feel that she is so worthy that her husband will step out of his comfort zone and be romantic. A husband, too, has similar dreams. He loves to feel as if his wife loves him enough to be his lover rather than just a mother to his children. A marriage can be in trouble when the couple gets to the point where spouses refer to each other as "Mom" and "Dad" rather than by other, more personal names. This may indicate the role that each has fallen into. The parenting role will eventually end as the kids leave home. That role will become obsolete. The role of husband and wife will continue, and these are the roles that need to be worked on the most.

It's a Balance of Cherish and Cheer

The husband is supposed to work on seeing the need for relationship that his wife has. Then he's to step out of what he's comfortable doing and meet that need. It's his sacrifice.

The wife is to submit to the needs of her husband. She's to be his partner and balance that with his need to be respected.

This might not be easy, but cheering for him is her ultimate submission to God's plan for marriage. Cheering for him means she is to be his greatest supporter. She needs to encourage him and make sure he knows his wife is behind him no matter what.

One wife asked, "Why do you think God set up the marriage relationship like this?" The counselor responded with, "I don't know. But I don't know a lot of things. It's my job to assume God knows what He's doing and then submit to His plan."

If you want to see how your relationship is doing in the area of the self-esteem of your spouse, there's a litmus test. Ask yourself these questions: "Does my spouse seem to be happy and feel fulfilled in the fact he or she is loved? Does my spouse seem to enjoy spending large blocks of time with me?" If so, perhaps it's because his or her self-esteem needs are being enhanced by your relationship. A husband might ask, "Does my wife feel cherished?" A wife could ask, "Do I cheer for my husband, or do I spend my time criticizing him?"

Summary

1. Each spouse has a great opportunity, even a responsibility, to enhance the self-esteem of his or her partner.

2. Women are more sophisticated in the area of relationship; hence their self-esteem needs are enhanced by an in-depth marriage relationship. If they perceive and hear that they are cherished, they feel valuable.

3. Most men haven't had the opportunity to grow in the area of deep relationships. However, their self-esteem is enhanced by feeling as if they are respected by their spouses.

4. Both genders battle for self-esteem in our culture. Self-esteem needs can best be met if each spouse steps out of his or her own comfort zone and meets the needs of the spouse.

Discussion Questions

1. In what area is your spouse's self-esteem low? How can you begin building it?

2. As a husband, how do you communicate to your spouse that she is adored and cherished by you? How can you improve?

3. As a wife, how do you communicate to your husband that you appreciate and respect him for who he is?

Further Readings on This Topic

What Wives Wish Their Husbands Knew about Women, James Dobson, Tyndale House.

Dr. Dobson Answers Your Questions, James Dobson, Tyndale House.

The Language of Love, Gary Smalley and John Trent, Focus on the Family.

For Better or for Best, Gary Smalley, Zondervan.

Lonely Husbands, Lonely Wives, Dennis Rainey, Word.

21

Practice Safe Marriage: Use Protection

I just don't know what happened," Matt's story began. "Two years ago Rhonda and I celebrated our tenth wedding anniversary. Well, I guess you wouldn't really say celebrated. We weren't getting along very well, even back then. Rhonda was mad at me because we didn't do anything special for our tenth anniversary, so we weren't talking.

"Our marriage was just boring. You know, no passion. I almost had to beg for sex, and that got very old. I never intended to have an affair with a girl at work, it just happened. Then I spent a year thinking I was in love with this girl. For that year I thought she was the perfect one for me. I left Rhonda, only to find out a year later that I'm still unhappy. Maybe it wasn't Rhonda. Maybe it was me. Who knows? I do know this, however. A few nights of what I thought were passion have now sparked a lifetime of agony and loneliness."

How Does It Happen?

Affairs are often predictable. There are some factors that open the door to an affair, but husbands and wives are left to make the final decision for themselves as to whether or not they are going to walk through that door. Some may be more predisposed to extramarital affairs than others, but it's still avoidable, no matter who the person is. When looking at this marital cancer it is helpful to seek some of the underlying factors.

Immaturity

Immaturity plays a big part in marital infidelity. Some individuals are so immature that they go into adulthood still responding to life like adolescents. Their immaturity allows them the excuse of giving in to temptation. A rebellious teen-age attitude is one that does not want to be restrained by commitments. A person with that kind of attitude wants to do what he wants to do when he wants to do it. (It should be said here that the "he" is being used as a generic term. I have seen just as many woman as men who have had extramarital affairs.) In this situation a person feels that if he wants to do it, to have an affair, then he ought to be able to do it. If it "feels good," that's license enough.

Many children grow up in homes where their parents indulge them; anything they want they get. They don't have to wait for something or earn it. If they just ask or demand, their busy parents will get it for them rather than train the child in the character quality of self-discipline. These same children grow up to be people who demand this instant gratification of extramarital affairs. Discipline in the home could have a great impact on the marital commitments of a child when he grows up.

Conflicts

Conflicts are inevitable, but when they go unresolved, conflicts become erosive. Oftentimes the constant nagging of a conflict can erode the marital foundation to the point that a husband and wife don't even like being around each other.

That was Matt's story. He was so self-centered that he failed to hear his wife's dream of making their anniversary special. He didn't want to spend the money. After all, it was really just another anniversary. This was just the final straw after many other, more significant conflicts. Matt was self-centered, and Rhonda gave up. Two big mistakes.

A woman at the office became an emotional comfort zone for Matt. At first they just talked. Then they went out to lunch together and, for the first time in years, Matt was able to communicate with a female without hearing sarcastic comments. He felt like somebody.

Conflicts need to be dealt with. If not, the marriage can start to erode. If the conflict is not dealt with, the more mature spouse must choose not to shut down the relationship and attempt to punish the other party. That person must keep trying.

Unmet Needs

More times than not, it is the woman who seems to get trapped by the land mine of unmet needs. She is so desperate for a relationship that she becomes very vulnerable to the attention of a nice person. Perhaps he's just a man she met at church who talks to her and actually takes time to listen to her. But before she realizes it, she's in trouble. That's probably how so many pastors find themselves in extramarital affairs. By profession, the pastor listens to the pain of a woman in his church. She thinks he's wonderful because he's so sensitive. He, too, needs someone to think he's wonderful. The trap is set, and they both fall into it, together.

Affairs Are Marketed

If a person today spends much time at all watching the television sitcoms, he could easily be trapped into believing that he or she is obviously missing something. There are so many sexual innuendoes. There's also so much instant passion. Two people meet, they go back to one person's apartment, and passion takes over—all in just a matter of twenty minutes. And, of course, it all happens with no consequences. We've been brainwashed into believing that the chief end of humanity is to find passion, even if it's outside of marriage.

The marketers have also worked on another area of our attitudes toward life, telling us "You deserve this." How many times have I heard it said by men and women justifying affairs, "I deserved more than I was getting out of my marriage." We've been marketed so long to believe that we deserve better and we should be able to have it now, without working too hard for it, either.

This is an incredibly destructive attitude that has permeated our society. Actually, we have already received much more than we deserve. In the words of R. C. Sproul, in *Holiness of God*, "Do you want what you deserve? You deserve hell!"

Protecting Your Marriage

If extramarital affairs are such a subtle and corrosive force in today's marriage it would seem that we would want to take steps to protect ourselves from them. "Oh, that's ridiculous!" one husband said at the beginning of a seminar. "I don't need to get paranoid about this whole thing. I'll just decide that I'm not going to let it happen."

I didn't do that with rust. When I bought my new car I had rust protector put on it. I wasn't paranoid. It just seemed like a good investment. I wanted to do the best I could to prevent rust. How much more true that is for marriage! An ounce of protection will go a long way.

There are steps you can take to "affair-proof" your marriage. J. Allen Peterson's *The Myth of Greener Grass* is the classic in the area of dealing with and preventing extramarital affairs. It is a must for every home. It will also give guidance to a couple who wants to help a friend whose marriage is in the midst of this cancer.

Step One

Don't compare your marriage to anyone else's marriage. Things are not as they appear. We are all good at imagining how other couples relate to each other. Many times other people believe that Rosemary must surely be fortunate to be married to someone like me since I speak on marriage and the needs of women. On top of that, I'm a counselor and know how to listen. As they get to know me, they quickly realize just how long-suffering Rosemary truly is! Don't try to compare your marriage to anyone else's. It's not comparable.

Step Two

Look at the friends around you, not to compare, but to see if there are any traps waiting to open up. So many times counselors hear people say, "I can't believe this has happened, and he's run off with my best friend, too."

We live in a culture that thinks flirting is cute. Many people with whom we socialize could be more dangerous than we imagine. Heeding warnings is often difficult for the man. I remember a time, years ago, when Rosemary and I were at a party. A woman was spending a lot of time asking me questions about my profession. When we left the party that night Rosemary commented about the fact that this woman had monopolized my time, and Rosemary didn't think that was wise. She went so far as to say that she thought I should be careful of this particular woman.

In the past I had asked my wife to help me deal with situations like these, but her comments this particular night caught me off guard. Rosemary's comments attacked my male ego, and I responded like an adolescent. "I can handle myself," was the basic way I responded to my wife's advice. This woman was giving me some attention and asking questions that I was able to answer. It was a boost for my ego. But my wife was right. We need to give each other the respect to take each other's advice. We are there to protect each other, and my wife was able to see things that I was temporarily blinded to.

Step Three

Beware of lowering your own inhibitions. There are many things in this culture that may be acceptable to the society we live in but are incredibly destructive to the marriage commitment. These are things that cause us to lower our inhibitions or walls. These are things that cause men, especially, to fantasize about other women. Some magazines or videos are cancers to the thought life. I know, you're just reading those magazines for the articles and interviews! Protect your eyes from things that could cause you to become disenchanted with your marriage.

Step Four

Set boundaries for yourself. This is getting more and more difficult in this day and age. It is still possible to set boundaries that will protect your marriage; they are just different from marriage to marriage and from person to person. I choose not to have lunch alone with another woman. If through business it becomes mandatory for me to meet at lunch with a woman, I take along another colleague so that there are three of us. Everyone's boundaries may be different, and many reading this section may think it's archaic even to be talking about boundaries. I don't want to risk straying from my marriage commitment for any reason. Even if it may cause some to think that I'm overreacting, it's worth the risk, especially in a society where extramarital affairs are rampant.

Protect your marriage. But you must do it in a way that does not smother your spouse. One spouse cannot hold on so tightly to the other that the restricted spouse becomes strangled. Protect your marriage without imposing a lot of restrictions on your spouse. Restrict yourself in a way that protects your heart.

Step Five

Start your own affair at home. What is it that's exciting about extramarital affairs? There's intrigue and spontaneity. There's also a lot of thought that goes into the relationship. The two people involved in an affair spend time planning where they are going to meet and when. If a married couple spent that much time working on their own marriage, they'd be much happier and feel less guilty.

"It took me a long time to realize that I wasn't really having an affair with the other woman," Matt said. "One day I realized that I was having an affair with the excitement. I thought I was in love with her. But then I realized that I was having an affair with the affair." Well said. It takes a long time for people to wake up and realize that if they put the effort it would take to have an affair into their own marriage, they'd be ecstatic about their marriage.

A friend of mine is a pilot. He often flies a route from a northern city, lays over in Miami, and then six hours later continues the flight to South America. Six hours isn't enough time for my friend to get in his car and drive to his home in Fort Lauderdale, so he just stays there at the airport and waits.

His wife, however, decided that she was going to have an affair with her husband. She started going to the Miami airport on the days when he was to lay over there. She rented a room at the airport hotel and had her husband paged. They were having an affair with each other. My friend said it was the first time he ever got excited about landing at Miami Airport. He wasn't going to accept the FAA waving him off to come in for another pass at the runway. He was going to land on the first pass. I know of few marriages that are as happy as theirs. That's because they put the planning efforts of an affair into their own marriage.

Protect your marriage from intrusion from the outside. At the same time, don't take your marriage for granted. Have an affair with your spouse.

Summary

1. Extramarital affairs are often signs of immaturity.

2. Unmet needs, unresolved conflict, and parental indulgence are all factors that can lead to extramarital affairs. But they're not excuses.

3. A couple can choose to protect their marriage from an extramarital affair.

4. The greatest way to protect a marriage from extramarital affairs is to have an affair at home.

Discussion Questions

1. Are there any areas where you are leaving your marriage vulnerable? Are there any areas where you feel your spouse is leaving the marriage vulnerable?

2. In what ways can you better protect your marriage?

3. Is there anything in your life that has lowered your inhibitions?

4. What can you do to bring excitement and spontaneity back into your relationship?

Further Reading on This Topic

The Myth of Greener Grass, J. Allen Peterson, Tyndale House.

22

Third-Party Intervention

I know I should have come for help sooner, but I felt funny," Margie said as she sat in the counselor's office weeping. "How do you know when it's time to go for counseling? How do you know where or who to go to? The fact that Bill refused to come for counseling made me feel like it would be foolish to come alone. I guess I wondered if it was even okay to get counseling in the first place!"

Margie isn't alone in her questions about the whole counseling process. Many people wonder about utilizing the services of a counselor. Many others have heard horror stories about people going to counselors and their situation got even worse than it was before they went for help. These are questions that need to be answered. Margie didn't seek answers to her questions; she just left them as questions. Consequently, Bill had left home and he was filing for divorce.

Is It Okay to Use the Services of a Counselor?

In past generations, couples were surrounded by families and communities who watched them grow up. As that generation grew up, got married, and began to be in need of help with their marriage relationships, they knew who to go sit with and talk to. "Aunt Ellie, could I come over and talk to you about something?" That would be the way the quasi-counseling appointment would be approached. It was with a person in the community who probably wasn't even a blood aunt, but a trusted, wiser friend.

Counseling and help with family relations has been going on forever. It is apparent that Nathan was a very valuable counselor to King David. At David's lowest point, Nathan was able to confront the king, and this counseling session, done with a metaphor, saved David from his own destruction (see 2 Samuel 12).

Never before has there been a society set in such conflict. The culture isn't even sure how to define what a family is anymore. As a Christian, I would think I know that definition, and yet I see many with whom I worship that define the term *family* using different parameters. This is a time when the services of a counselor can be used to work through the difficult issues of our times that might be polluting a marriage.

Many new "plagues" or sins have been revealed in recent times. These sins, such as sexual abuse, spouse abuse, and substance abuse, aren't new; they're just more rampant than ever before. There are counselors who are trained to help confront or deal with these difficulties, difficulties that go beyond what Aunt Ellie was or is prepared to give advice about.

In this age of specialized ministry, the services of a counselor can be a blessing. A counselor can help offer a set of binoculars to help a person work through some of life's difficult terrain. A counselor will never be able to lead the way or supply the map. That's far too much responsibility to give to someone else. The actual journey must be walked by the individual with God. Unfortunately, there are many counselees who have made or allowed their counselors to become a god. (Notice that this is a small "g" god, not worthy of the position of the capital "G.") Only our Lord can take us on the actual walk through the wilderness journeys of life. A counselor can help us look at the map and the options, but the counselor should direct us toward the Godly path.

How Do You Know When It's Time to Seek Counseling?

There are significant conflicts and there are insignificant, short-term conflicts. When an important relationship encounters a significant conflict that is not being resolved, it is then time to seek outside help. On the other hand, it might well be that a conflict is not significant enough to cause long-term difficulty in the relationship. The fact that a husband and wife are different and approach day-to-day functions differently is to be expected. Her dreams and expectations about marriage are different than his. She didn't expect that her husband would come home at night and leave his clothes on the bedroom floor. She has enough things to do without having to figure out how to deal with his mess. On the other hand, he grew up expecting a little different kind of dinner on the table every night. His mother was home all day.

These are unmet expectations that we all need to adjust to, rather than use a counselor's time and the counselee's money to try and change a spouse. These are areas where each spouse must learn compromise for the good of the marriage.

There are other marital conflicts, however, that a couple must resolve, such as differing opinions on moral issues or the way one spouse treats another spouse. These can become tremendous roadblocks to marital growth. When an issue has become so big that it interferes with the marriage relationship, it might be time to seek counseling.

"We had a tremendous argument this weekend, and I need to come and talk to a counselor, *today*." This was the way the phone conversation went as a caller talked to the receptionist at Sheridan House Counseling Center. "There are no openings for counseling today. Could a counselor call you back today and talk to you for a few minutes and then set an appointment?" "Okay, but please have someone call back."

The counselor called back and spent time talking with a very distraught wife. The issue was football and the amount of time her husband was dedicating to watching the games. She was very disappointed. The counselor encouraged her to talk to her husband about her disappointment. "I've tried," she said, "but I'm wasting my breath!"

The counselor set an appointment to see the lady, or the couple, in two weeks and she was told the counseling fee. "Two weeks!" this wife all but yelled into the phone. "I can't take this for another two weeks!" This distraught wife was told that the next available time for her would be in two weeks. If in the meantime, she was able to talk to her husband and the two of them could deal with this particular issue, she was free to cancel the appointment.

Sometimes issues that seem paramount at the time will not seem so significant when given a few days to think through the difficulty or talk about it. This counselor assessed the gravity of the situation. Was it the football or was it something far deeper? Was it life threatening or was it an overreaction? Did this couple really need counseling or did they need a deadline by which they needed to talk about hurt feelings? A week later the lady called back to thank the counselor and say that they didn't really need to keep the appointment. The counselor once again returned the call to make sure things really were better and to reassure her that his services were available in the future if help was needed. Counseling is not to be used to deal with weekend arguments. It is to be used for issues that are ongoing and that block the marriage from the growing process that should never stop.

The Sexual Barometer

One rule of thumb as to the severity of the problem is the sexual barometer. While this is not true in every relationship, it is often an indicator in many marriages. If the sexual intimacy is being interrupted, then there may be a larger conflict that is not resolved. If one spouse is finding it difficult to respond sexually to the other spouse, that may be a red flag that there is an ongoing problem in another area of the relationship.

Choosing a Counselor

There are many important factors that must be studied when selecting a counselor. Is he or she licensed? What do they charge? Do they take insurance? What is the counselor's philosophy of life? Are they trained in marriage counseling or another area?

These are significant questions that many people fail to ask when looking for a counselor. For some reason counselors have a mind-set that they just need to set an appointment and all these pertinent questions will work themselves out. A counselor is very similar to an appliance repairman. He works for you, not the other way around. Just as I would call Alber's Appliances to ask if they worked on Maytags, the counselee needs to call the counselor and ask questions. If the counselor is too busy to return your call to talk for five minutes, call elsewhere.

The yellow pages is not the place to start the search. The first place to ask for help in locating a competent counselor is the church that you attend. Most pastors and their staff will have already done their homework, and have a list of local counselors they can tell you about. An additional way of locating a counselor is to call Focus on the Family in Colorado Springs (1-800-A-FAMILY). Focus has located counselors in most cities in America.

Call the counselor's office and ask that the counselor call you back so you can talk about the counselor's approach to counseling. Write on a piece of paper the things that are important to you. If the counselor is not able to answer the questions in a way that you think is satisfactory, ask why. There may be a reason that the counselor is not yet licensed; he may have an answer for that. There may be a reason that she doesn't take insurance.

Where does the counselor go to church? The counselor's philosophy of life is a very significant factor. Otherwise, the counselor might not understand the counselee's commitment level and ability to forgive. How does he feel about divorce? Is he a Christian? Collect the answers, pray about the decision, and then call back to set the appointment. The counselee should make sure that he or she is setting an appointment with the person that he is requesting rather than with someone else in the practice.

Don't use this phone call for a mini-counseling session. That's not fair to the counselor and it will discourage the counselor from returning your calls in the future. Ask the questions and decide whether or not to set the appointment with that particular counselor.

"But I can't believe how much it costs!" is a comment that many counselors have heard their clients make. I recently had to have my air-conditioner worked on. The repairman charged sixty dollars an hour. I'm sure he didn't get all that; he obviously has overhead and other staff back in his office to pay. I paid it because it was worth it to get my air-conditioner repaired. How sad that many people will pay to get help repairing their things, but not their families. A counselor has to eat, too. Even if the counseling center is a ministry, there are still salaries to pay. Is a marriage worth it? Don't wait too long simply because of the money.

The Rust Can Overtake You

Years ago we bought a little used Volkswagen bug. It needed a lot of work, but it got us where we needed to go. One of my friends, an engineer, commented on the rust on the side of our VW one day. "Bob, if you don't take care of that soon it will . . ." and he went on to give me a great dissertation on the impact of rust left unchecked. I didn't want to spend the time or money, nor did I want to hear my friend's dissertation. I knew one day I'd get to it.

A few months later, as we were driving to school, the bottom fell out of the little VW. It just couldn't take the stress any longer. It was something I should have dealt with, but I waited too long. It ended up costing me a lot more money than it would have if I had taken care of the problem right away. The comparison is obvious. Don't wait until the bottom falls out of your marriage. If your spouse won't go for counseling, go alone.

Let the counselor help you plan how to deal with a spouse who is unreceptive. But go for help.

Summary

1. Marriage counselors are needed today more than ever before. They offer specialized help in a society that is often confused about marital issues and boundaries.

2. Counseling should be sought when there is a conflict significant enough to disrupt the marriage relationship for a long period of time.

3. Interview the counselor. The counselor works for you, not the other way around.

4. Decide ahead of time the questions that you want to ask the counselor when you interview the counselor on the phone.

5. Don't wait until the rust takes over!

Discussion Questions

1. Do you have issues in your marriage that are like rust? Are they solvable? Can you talk about them or do you need third-party intervention?

2. If you feel a counselor would be beneficial, what are the questions you need to ask the counselor when calling for an appointment? Make a list.

3. Are these marital disagreements that can be overlooked as something that happens because we are all different? Or are they issues that are making it difficult for you to respond to your spouse?

Part 6

It's a Matter of
Doing Love

23

Love vs. Feelings

I don't know when it went away," Lonnie began his story in the marriage counselor's office. "We got married a few years ago and it felt great. I mean, we were really in love. But now I just don't have any feelings for Rebecca anymore. That's the best way to describe it; the feeling is gone."

Lonnie came to the marriage counselor to appease his wife, Rebecca. He didn't want to be there. Instead, he wanted out of the marriage. He got to the point where he thought he had made a mistake. As far as he was concerned, if there weren't any feelings, there wasn't any reason to be married.

A Culture of Feelers

At some point in our culture we really bought the philosophy, "If it feels good, do it." Without realizing it, we began to be controlled by our feelings. That is also true for our lack of feelings. You ask someone why he called in sick to work when he was obviously not sick. "Oh, I just didn't feel like going in," is not an uncommon answer.

We are a culture of "feelers." If something doesn't feel good or nice, we don't want to do it. It doesn't really matter whether it's good for us or the right thing to do. Feelings have become an overwhelming power in our decision-making process.

This power of feelings has become a major factor in marriage relationships, as well. People get married and for the first few months they operate on feelings.

Steinmetz and Wiese, in their book *Everything You Need to Know to Stay Married and Like It*, have indicated that every marriage goes through very distinct stages.

The first stage of a marriage can be labeled the Honeymoon Stage. This first stage is a period that can last for days, weeks, months or even years. It's the period where a couple is operating on feelings. They put little feelers out to attempt to have their needs met. This is a time of very high expectations.

Expectations

It's only natural to come into a marriage with high expectations. Each person has waited so long and dreamed about what a marriage will mean to him or to her. Actually, each person has dreamed about what marriage will do for him or her, personally.

It doesn't take long for those expectations to be burst. Over a period of time the feelings wear off. Actually, these are only feelings of newness. The powerful "feelings" a couple experiences could also be their strong physical attraction. When familiarity sets in, that powerful physical attraction sometimes wanes. When these things happen, a couple might fear that they are losing these "all-important feelings." Each spouse must look at his (or her) spouse and realize that this person is only human.

"Before we were married," Lonnie said to the counselor, "I didn't notice her strange idiosyncrasies. It didn't bother me the way she did things. In fact, I didn't even notice they were weird; I thought they were cute. Now the things she does make me crazy. I don't know. Either I thought I could change her or I didn't think it would bother me."

The feelings that he had for her weren't carrying him over the hurdle of accepting her differences. What he used to think was cute now got on his nerves. His feelings were controlling his attitude toward his wife.

Responding to Feelings

Feelings or the loss of feelings must be dealt with. Unfortunately, either a person controls his feelings or his feelings control him. Lonnie was choosing to let his feelings control him. That's one response to feelings. There are others.

Adolescent Response. Anyone who has had teenagers knows that their whole life is controlled by feelings. They are so hopelessly under the thumb of their feelings that a parent must feel sorry for them.

Most people don't believe that feelings are that flippant. Yet people can walk into a movie theater in a depressed mood, then see an exciting, uplifting movie and walk out of the theater feeling great. They just allowed the movie to manipulate their feelings.

Whether we realize it or not, we choose our feelings. Lonnie was allowing the adolescent in him to take over. He was making a subconscious choice to pull his feelings away from his wife.

A person like Lonnie doesn't really know what it is to love a person. He thinks that love is a feeling of ecstasy. He figures that since he doesn't really have those feelings for Rebecca, then he must not be "in love" anymore. Actually Lonnie is in love, but he is in love with meeting his own needs. To him, love is finding ways to make Lonnie feel good.

The result is a very short-term gratification choice. Someone else in his office could make him feel good for a moment in time, and he could choose to have an affair. Lonnie is letting feelings, which could change as frequently as the weather, be in control of his life.

Grin and Bear It. Other people are far more disciplined than Lonnie. They would never let their feelings stray to another person and if they did, they would never admit to it.

These people think that love is a commitment, and that's all there is to it.

They're right to a point. Love is a commitment. But grin-and-bear-it people just decide that feelings are something to be suppressed. They believe that feelings are for newlyweds and that they are now under marital obligations. They don't realize that feelings are great, when directed in the right direction.

Grin and bear it was the response to marriage that was made by many people married prior to 1960. Marriage allowed them to have children and not be lonely. When their feelings for their spouses died, they just buried the thought of ever having feelings again. If feelings toward others came into their consciousness, they did their best to get them under control. This generation was almost afraid of feelings. Feelings could be dangerous, since they could lead to getting hurt or doing things that were out of control. They got married with feelings and then let the feelings go.

The danger of this kind of relationship is that it gets very dry. People in these marriages become very vulnerable to other relationships. If they ever let themselves go by responding to another person, they think it's that other person they have feelings for. They don't realize that it's really just their desire to experience feeling something for another person that is exciting to them.

It's difficult to turn this cycle around in a marriage, especially a marriage that has lived for several years with feelings buried. It can be done, however. Old habits can be broken if a person chooses to do so. I will never forget finishing a marriage seminar at Bethany Presbyterian Church in Fort Lauderdale. We challenged couples to come back to the altar to rededicate themselves to their marriages. One of the first couples to start to the altar was a couple who had been married for sixty-two years. One was using a walker, and the other had to be helped. They wanted to change the way they had been responding to each other. It was a very moving time for everyone at the conference. We all learned from the things this couple said. It's never too late to change.

Choosing to Feel. The healthy way to handle feelings is to use them. Some people are used by their feelings. Their feelings control them and they move from thought to thought, or person to person, according to the fickleness of their feelings. People who understand feelings are neither controlled by their feelings nor do they suppress their feelings. Instead, they discipline their feelings. They decide where they will allow their feelings to go.

Sitting at lunch with a friend one day, we began talking about one of the men we knew who had gotten involved in an extramarital affair. We both knew that this man only *thought* he was "in love" but he really didn't know what love was.

"It's his irresponsible handling of feelings," my friend began. "At first Bill was the picture of control and discipline. He wouldn't let his feelings get out of control for anything. In fact, he wouldn't even express them. He was very legalistic about anything that smacked of a lack of control.

"After years of showing no feeling to his wife or anybody, Bill let go one day and slowly started expressing feelings toward our secretary. Now they're having an affair. Bill doesn't know how to feel. It's like he just fired his feelings out indiscriminately and shot someone."

When I asked my friend what he meant by "shot someone," he went on to beautifully describe the handling of feelings. "Feelings are like bullets. Most guys shower their wives with these 'feeling bullets' during the first few months of marriage. Then they put the gun back in the holster. After a while they wake up one day and decide they're tired of not feeling. They're lonely. They pull out that gun and shoot. Unfortunately, they shoot in the wrong direction. They could choose to shoot their feeling bullets at their wives, but they don't."

They don't because it would be harder to start shooting the feelings at their wives. Perhaps there have been conflicts or arguments that would make the husband feel too humbled to start shooting feelings toward his wife. She might find it difficult to start shooting her feelings his way because she has so many unmet expectations. She's been rejected before and doesn't want to go through it again. It's just easier (though adolescent) to shoot the feelings at someone new.

"What do you mean by 'shooting feelings'?" I asked my very wise friend. He responded by saying, "Let's say I see an attractive woman walk by me while we're sitting here for lunch. I can choose to continue looking and begin to think about her. Or I can choose to look away and say to myself, 'What can I do that would bless Gloria's (his wife) day today?' Sometimes I even say a quick prayer, 'Lord teach me something I can do for my wife today.'"

My friend immediately brought his thoughts back to his marriage. He pulled his thoughts and his feelings back home. Thinking about doing something special for his wife, he stayed excited about the relationship. He decided to use his feelings to be a blessing to his wife's life. My friend also went on to say that there was a time in his life when he no longer felt a strong sexual desire for his wife. He said that during that time he actually prayed, "Lord, help me to lust after my wife again."

They have a great marriage, but it's by choice. My friend has decided to express his feelings in one direction and one direction only. He keeps that gun pointed at his wife. Love means that you choose to keep your feelings flowing toward your spouse and you choose to do it abundantly. Feelings don't control love. Love must be the disciplining force that controls the trigger on the feelings gun. It's a choice, but it's a choice that must be made. Either you choose to control your feelings, or they will direct your path, just like they do an adolescent's.

Lonnie was helped to put a safety on his feelings gun as far as the other woman in his office was concerned. He worked hard and he was able to stop pointing his feelings in the direction of the other woman. The difficulty came in pointing and releasing his feelings toward his wife. It was a constant daily effort to try to express love and do things for his wife.

She didn't help matters as she went from rejecting him one week to smothering him the next. It took a year of effort, but they are now happier than they ever believed possible. It was summed up by his wife when she said, "I find it hard to believe that he's the same man. I'm happier than I ever dreamed I could be." Lonnie had refocused his feelings gun and fired.

Summary

1. Feelings, left uncontrolled, can be very flippant, even dangerous.

2. Feelings must be controlled and directed.

3. Feelings can't be overlooked or suppressed or they can explode and cause a lot of damage.

4. Feelings are a great way to direct your love toward your spouse, but they must be consciously directed.

Discussion Questions

1. How do you respond to feelings in your marriage?

2. What can you do to protect the direction you point your feelings?

3. What can you do to rekindle those old feelings you had for one another?

4. When is the most recent time you had great feelings toward your spouse? What was it about that situation that brought out your feelings?

Further Reading on This Topic

Everything You Need to Know to Stay Married and Like It, Bernard Wiese and Urban G. Steinmetz, Zondervan.

24

Deciding to Forgive

But she hasn't asked me to forgive her," Ron explained. "How can I forgive Linda if she hasn't come to me to ask for forgiveness?"

That's a pretty standard thought process. Ron's wife had done something to their marriage relationship that he felt was a major violation, and it was. He felt that he wasn't going to renew their relationship or even try to mend it until she came to him and asked for forgiveness. As a result, they were living in separate homes. As far as he was concerned the first move was up to her.

There are many people in that very same situation. They allow themselves to be controlled by another person. "I can't do anything right now," one lady said. "How can I deal with my ex-husband until he apologizes for what he has done to our lives and the lives of our children? I'll never be able to forget this and that means I just don't think I'll ever be able to forgive him!"

Forgiving vs. Forgetting

It's a very common mistake to assume that these two words, which are often linked so closely, are inseparable. They might often be linked together, but *forgiving* and *forgetting* are two very different areas of responsibility. Forgetting a hurt or injustice that has taken place is not the responsibility of the recipient. The ex-wife who said that she could never forget what her husband had done was right. She, by herself, would never be able to forget what had been done. She can take the first steps toward forgetting, however.

The actual process of forgetting will take time. Over a long period the hurt will eventually fade from her memory if she takes the proper steps. Eventually she could get to the point where her thoughts about the incident and pain are as if they happened to someone else. It will be a memory, but one that is no longer painful and vivid.

God is the one who heals memories. In Genesis, Joseph was the great forgiver of the Old Testament. His brothers had done an unspeakable thing to him by selling him into slavery. Yet, years later, he was able to say that he had forgotten the pain. Though the pain of this act may have been hourly for quite some time, he finally reached the point where he named his first child Manasseh, and at the naming of this child he said, "It is because God has made me forget all my trouble . . ." (Gen. 41:51).

God had used time to heal Joseph's memory of the pain. Joseph was able to forget because he trusted God with this pain. The ability to forget is *God's responsibility*. But there is a necessary step that must be taken in order to forget, and that's why forgive and forget are linked together.

Forgetting is God's job, but forgiving is the individual's responsibility. The power company has the responsibility to supply my home with the power that will illuminate the light bulb in my study. I pay them to do that, and they guarantee that they will. However, if I don't turn the switch on it will never happen. They can send all the power they want and the light will never illuminate the room. It's not the power company's fault; it's my fault. I never held up my end of the bargain. I didn't choose to turn the switch on.

The switch to turn on forgetting is to choose to forgive. "That's ridiculous!" Ron said. "How can I just choose to forgive? I don't feel like forgiving." Isn't it amazing how we want so desperately to get rid of the pain and yet we don't want to do what's necessary to get rid of it? It's a matter of choosing to get rid of the pain. That means choosing to forgive so that God can help you forget.

Controlled by the Other Person

The first step is to choose. Whether Ron wanted to or not, he had to decide that he was going to forgive his wife, Linda. If he didn't choose to do that, then every time he thought about her he would get into a bad mood. Every time he saw her, saw something of hers, or was reminded of her, it would cause him to feel pain and anger. Ultimately he would be choosing to be a very bitter man. In effect, he would remain under Linda's control. Anything to do with Linda would cause Ron to change into a bitter man. The mere mention of her name by a friend already caused the countenance of his face to change.

"How can she still control me like this?" Ron asked. "I refuse to even talk to her anymore and yet it's like she has a power over me. I'm fine until I think about her. Then I change into a bitter old man."

A person who makes the decision to forgive the other person is deciding to no longer be controlled by that other person. That person will no longer be allowed to control his moods. Ron felt he was a yo-yo being thrown up and down by a power that Linda had over him. It was causing him to become very bitter. And the bitterness and anger were now taking over. He was being controlled by them.

There is a more significant reason to choose to forgive. Our Lord tells us that if we refuse to forgive those who sin against us, our Lord will refuse to forgive us. "For if ye forgive men their trespasses, your heavenly Father will forgive you" (see Matt. 6:14–15 KJV).

In order for God to work in a person's life, that person must first forgive. This is a prerequisite to the privilege of having God work in our lives. We all must forgive. If I live with bitterness in my heart and anger toward a person who has done something to me, then this verse indicates that God will do nothing until I have dealt with that attitude, until I have done something about my bitterness.

"Do you mean that I have to forgive Linda even if she doesn't come and ask for forgiveness?" Ron asked. The answer to this question is that God will not hold you accountable for another person's disobedience. You shouldn't have to sit around waiting for that other person to come to you and ask forgiveness. Some people would wait a lifetime, and that wouldn't be fair. God doesn't make your attitude and relationship to Him dependent on another person. He wants you to function independently of that other person. "Yes, Ron," the counselor answered. "You must choose to forgive Linda even if she never asks for it. That's your job before God."

Isn't it amazing how easy it is to choose to do that with our children? When my children do something wrong, I teach them to come back to me and apologize. When they are little, they come back with the proper words, but certainly not the proper attitude. "Sorry," they blurt, but only because they are told to say it. But we forgive our children; forgiveness is not contingent upon their asking. We make them say they're sorry because that's part of proper training, but in fact we have already forgiven them.

Somehow we quite naturally can choose to forgive our babies before they ever ask. It's important to transfer this to the way we handle the adults around us. We must chose to forgive.

Christ hung on the cross for my sins. Centuries before I even asked for forgiveness He said, "Father, forgive them." He already paid the price for my sins; I just had to choose to accept the forgiveness. In His relationship toward me, He loved me before I first loved Him. He chose to forgive me before I asked.

Steps to Forgiving

Forgiveness is a choice, but it is also very difficult. It starts with prayer. It would be very difficult to choose to forgive a spouse who has continually wronged you, unless you have the

power of God behind the choice. The first step toward forgiving another person is to ask God to help in this effort.

Forgiveness is an attitude that one chooses to take toward
another person. No matter how bad it has been, the person
choosing to forgive is deciding to establish his or her own response to the situation and the other person. That response
needs to be totally apart from the response or interaction with
the person who is to be forgiven. It cannot be contingent. "I
seem to do okay until Linda starts to push my buttons. She
knows just what to do to make me furious."

The attitude needs to be one where the person will battle
the natural reaction of shooting back when being shot at. If a
person shoots back it means that the other person totally controls the situation. If Ron's ex-wife wanted to make him react
emotionally, she could because he let her.

A person who chooses to forgive is choosing to take on an
attitude that will give kindness for unkindness. This person will
not allow himself to be pulled down into the mud of bitterness.
Instead, he must choose a different attitude.

Ron found that he first needed to pray, "Father, I'm getting ready to meet with Linda. Please help me maintain an attitude of forgiveness no matter what she says."

Forgiveness requires a daily regrouping. After the umpteenth
time Ron failed at this, he had to decide that forgiving wasn't
a once-and-for-all process. He was learning something new,
and it had to be relearned daily. This is an attitude that has to
be concentrated on each day as if it is something relearned. In
Matthew 18:21–22, the Lord instructs us to forgive "seventy
times seven (kjv)." That implies that forgiveness is an ongoing
process that needs to be repeated numerous times.

When you break a leg, you have to learn to walk all over
again. Each day you realize you've made some mistakes, but you
also find you have made progress. You feel like you're getting
there. Then you go to sleep and let your leg be idle. The next
morning when you put your foot on the ground to test it, it
feels like you're having to start all over again. You think, *Will*

I ever walk right again? It takes an act of the will to keep trying to do it right.

Choosing to forgive is like that. First you take baby steps, then bigger steps, and then you fall; you feel like you'll never get it right. It takes an act of your will to find the progress. You decide that you and God will control your attitude rather than letting it be controlled by the comments of another person.

Forgiveness is an action more than just an attitude, however. If I am learning to forgive another person I must also decide to wish that person well. I must hope for his or her best. I must work on the thought that I don't want that person to fail and be punished for what he or she has done.

"Boy, does that sound wimpy!" Ron said as he looked at the floor. "Actually," the counselor responded, "that takes a tremendous amount of discipline—discipline to control your thoughts and natural reactions to Linda. Your natural reaction is to hope she fails so you can gloat. That's not forgiveness, that's revenge."

Ron's real quest was for the discipline to control his anger and thoughts so that he could not only wish for but try and help Linda in any way. But part of him wanted to make life miserable for her by making their joint decisions as difficult as possible. That wasn't choosing forgiveness.

Many people, after divorce or separation, choose to make the other person miserable by making the children's visitation situations a nightmare. Others find that when they choose to do it differently and forgive the person they get abused for it. The other person, the one being forgiven, takes advantage of the situation. The ex-spouse sees it as weakness and keeps the children out past their time. Forgiveness is not dependent on the other person's response to it. Nor is it dependent on the cooperation of the offending party. If either of these is happening, then once again the other person is drawing you back into the battle of bitterness.

Forgiveness is a choice that one person makes toward another. The attitude of forgiveness corresponds to an action that is taken toward the forgiven person's welfare. Once again it cannot be dependent on the way the other person responds.

Forgiveness is an independent act between you and God. Even if the other person does not come back after walking out on a marriage, or gets worse than before, it should not affect or provoke bitterness. Obviously this is easier said than done. As was said before, forgiveness takes a daily decision and effort. But forgiveness should not be an attitude and action taken in order to manipulate.

Ron said with all brokenness, "If I forgive Linda, do you think that she'll come back to me?" There is no way to answer that question. The other person's response to the fact that he or she is being forgiven is not the forgiver's responsibility. Forgiving is not a way of controlling someone. It is a way for the forgiver not to be controlled, however. Whether the forgiven person feels the forgiveness changes is between him or her and God.

The fact that a person chooses to forgive a spouse does not mean that he or she must endure abuse. Some spouses, choosing to forgive, think that it will cause their partners to change from an unacceptable lifestyle. That is not necessarily the case.

"If you really forgave me as you say, you'd let me come back home to live." Once again, it must be said that forgiveness is devoid of the other person's response. The choice is to forgive without condoning a sinful lifestyle. That may mean forgiving but refusing to let a spouse return home until changes have been made. A great book to help with this decision is *Love Must Be Tough* by Dr. James Dobson.

Forgiveness is contagious. No one enjoys being around a bitter, angry person. Yet our society today seems to foster bitter, angry attitudes. Most of the things we hear about are the negative things taking place around us. People don't spend time gossiping about the positive attributes of others.

An attitude of forgiveness is attractive and contagious. It is also a tremendous plus for the children of a household to be raised by a parent who has chosen to forgive the other spouse rather than be centered in on bitterness. The children very quickly see the contrast in attitudes.

It is a powerful force. When you forgive, you say to God, "This doesn't make sense, but because You have said I must do it, I will." It's trusting in the Lord and not leaning on your own understanding, but God's (see Prov. 3:5–6).

When a person chooses to trust God and respond to life according to what God says he or she should do, forgiveness becomes a powerful force. Then God will help not only the situation at hand but also the circumstances surrounding the situation. That includes the children as well as the ability to finally forget the pain. As always, God's plan is powerful, yet it operates in His timing.

Forgiveness is a demonstration of real love. Lou Ann had been deeply angry with her husband, Fred, for their whole marriage. It affected many areas of their relationship although she tried to be the kind of wife she knew she should be. Deep inside, however, she knew she was resentful of Fred.

One morning, while sitting alone, it all came to her. As a little girl she had dreamed of being a virgin when she got married. She had been very disciplined in that, even though she and Fred dated for three years before they got married. Six months before their marriage, however, Fred persuaded her to give in. "Since we're engaged now it really doesn't make any difference, anyway," Fred had said one night. In a night of passion Lou Ann had given up her dream and her virginity. She didn't realize how much this had made her resent Fred until she thought about it years later.

After this realization, Lou Ann tried to explain it to Fred. But he didn't understand how much this had affected their relationship. Lou Ann finally came to the point where she realized that she would have to forgive Fred even if he wasn't able to grasp the gravity of her pain. She had to decide to forgive and then act toward Fred accordingly. Forgetting the pain was a job that her Lord would have to help her with, over time.

Forgiving is the ultimate picture of love. It's not easy, it's not natural, and it's not a self-centered act. It's true love. It's forgiving the other person before he or she asks, because it's the right thing to do.

This plan holds true not only for the big things in life but also for the small day-to-day things. I can decide to be irritated by the fact that my wife leaves her shoes around the house, or I can decide to forgive her. An action coupled with that choice of forgiveness would be to pick them up for her and say nothing about it. Forgiveness is a key element to any relationship, but most especially a marriage. A person can choose to keep track of all the infractions or can choose to forgive and move on as if his or her spouse is perfect. It's a daily choice we each must make.

Ron had to spend a year working on this concept of forgiveness. One of the books that was the most help to him was *Forgive and Love Again* by John Nieder and Thomas Thompson. His wife, Linda, never came back during this time. But one day, sitting in the counselor's office, he made a very interesting statement, "You know, I'd go through all this pain again just to get where I am as far as understanding myself, getting rid of my bitter heart, and getting to know just how comforting my Lord is. Regardless of how this turns out, it was worth the journey."

Summary

1. Forgive and forget are two separate concepts.

2. A person must choose to forgive; the forgetting part will come with time and with God's help.

3. Forgiving is a daily discipline and attitude.

4. Forgiveness must be coupled with action.

5. The act of forgiving someone should be totally separate from the way that person responds or reacts.

Discussion Questions

1. How do you react when your spouse hurts or does something that is selfish?

2. What are some constructive steps you can use to deal with these irritations or deep hurts?

3. If you are in the process of forgiving, what act of forgiveness can you begin to demonstrate?

Further Reading on This Topic

Forgive And Love Again, John Nieder and Thomas Thompson, Harvest House.

Love Must Be Tough, James Dobson, Word.

25

What Is Love?

*I*t's inconceivable to me that Diane doesn't know that I love her!" That is a statement most marriage counselors have heard repeated countless times. They've heard it screamed by husbands and wept by wives. It's fitting that we end this book discussing the dilemma of just what it means to love.

Of all the issues concerning marriage, this is certainly the most abstract. It's easy to know what in-law problems are, and financial issues, and sexual conflicts. Once we identify a problem, we can deal with it. But the problem of loving another person, or feeling loved by a spouse, is complicated by the fact that we don't seem to be sure what real love is to begin with.

Love Is a Multi-Purpose Word

Almost once a day (a slight exaggeration on my part and since Rosemary rewrites these chapters she may change this) I seem to hear Rosemary say, "I love chocolate!" That's an interesting use of the word that we also use to describe our relationship with each other. Chocolate love must be a different kind of love than we use for each other. At least I hope it is. I'm sure if she were to get five or six bad pieces of chocolate in a row she wouldn't love chocolate anymore. I hope her love for me isn't contingent on constant good times. I would have failed the test long ago.

Our culture uses this word *love* for many different things.

In the case of chocolate it probably means *want* more than love. She wants chocolate as long as it's good.

We have other confusing phrases, such as "it was love at first sight." Actually that sounds more like a visual attraction or what we would call lust. Other couples have said that they "fell in love." What a funny way to put it. It sounds as if they were walking down a road and fell into a pothole. The couple had no choice; the hole was there and they just fell in. Love has to be something more than that.

Perhaps we misuse the word *love* and substitute it for words like *romance* or *infatuation*, things that we want or lust after. There must be more to love than this. Love must be a response that we choose to have toward another person, not toward a thing like a car or a house.

The Definition of Love

God must have decided that we would be floundering with this love definition, so He gave us a working definition. It's found in an often overused passage of Scripture. By overused, I mean many people may be overly acquainted with it and take it for granted. The passage, 1 Corinthians 13:4–8, provides the reader with a litmus test for maturity. This passage gives a quick summary of what it means to love a spouse. As I read it, I quickly find out whether I'm mature enough to give or take this kind of action toward another person. Love is an action toward another person rather than a feeling. Love is an action one chooses to take.

> Love is patient, love is kind. It does not envy, it does not boast, it is not proud. It is not rude, it is not self-seeking, it is not easily angered, it keeps no record of wrongs. Love does not delight in evil but rejoices with the truth. It always protects, always trusts, always hopes, always perseveres.
>
> Love never fails. (NIV)

As stated before, perhaps this passage may have become slick with use. So, to make it more personal and help me analyze whether I am choosing to love, I put my name in the passage and see if I am loving my spouse.

I am patient and kind. It's amazing how patient and kind we tend to act (and *act* is a good word here) toward people who don't even count. Take, for instance, the Sunday-morning experience. It's such a hassle to get the whole family into the car in order to get to church on time. Often I'm raising my voice, to put it mildly, in order to herd everyone toward the car. As we race out of the driveway, everyone is in a horrible mood because of the way I've treated them as we go off to worship.

I'm frowning, and sometimes lecturing, all the way to church, until we pull into the church parking lot. Then something happens when we pull into the lot. It's as if I miraculously come under a big vapor of mood-changing gas called the "aura of righteousness." Once on church property I'm smiling and waving. My kids must think I've totally lost my mind.

I'm now patient and kind. Why? There are people watching me. But there were people watching when I was home; my family was watching how I treat them. Why didn't that matter? It's because something happens when we know outsiders are watching. Perhaps that was the year I was "running" for deacon!

If I'm mature enough to love I must express that by choosing to be patient and kind to the ones I say I love.

I do not envy or boast; I am not proud or rude. Insecure people must always blow their own horns. They get jealous of what others have, even others who are close to them. One of the toughest things about being a little child is you have to learn to be happy for your brother or sister when something nice happens for him or her and not for you. Jealousy is a childish behavior that we are supposed to overcome by the time we reach adulthood. If I am an adult who wants to respond maturely toward my spouse, I will choose not to be envious and not to boast about "my" accomplishments. They are shared accomplishments.

Am I arrogant or rude when we are discussing something and I'm not getting my way? Even if I totally disagree with what my spouse is saying, how do I handle the disagreement? Am I violating the first part of this passage where it says to be kind and patient, waiting on the other person?

I am not self-seeking. This is a hard one. When I look at my marriage, do I look from the perspective of seeing what I can get out of it? If I choose to "do love," I must choose as my primary goal doing things for that person. This is true for our sexual relationship as well as every other aspect of our marriage. If I love, I do not seek my own happiness first.

I am not easily angered. It goes without saying that I must choose to be patient and calm in my response to difficult marital situations. That doesn't mean that we are to agree on everything. It doesn't even mean that we aren't supposed to debate. It means that we are to do it with the other person's feelings and welfare as a priority of the confrontation.

I do not keep a record of the wrongs. If I love, I choose to forget and not mention the wrongs or injustices that have already been discussed and resolved. God doesn't keep a record of the things I have asked forgiveness for. Do I have a greater right than God? Certainly not. When I choose to love my spouse, I choose to spend a lifetime of erasing the record of hurtful things that have been directed my way.

I do not delight in evil, but rejoice in the truth. What do I actually delight in? Do I delight in thinking only the best of things for my spouse? Do I delight in being a part of spiritual growth or "truth" with my marriage partner? Or do I sometimes seem to take delight in finding the things that my spouse does wrong, looking to see if she hasn't done something she was supposed to do so that I can delight in the fact that she forgot? That's delighting in evil rather than rejoicing in the relationship we can have through Christ. Analyze what you take delight in, in your thoughts toward your spouse. Is it something you get or take from your spouse, or is it a sacrifice you want to make for your spouse? How mature are you?

I always protect my love. This may be the portion of the love passage that has the greatest impact on me, personally. Do we protect our marriages from anything that would harm the relationships? Are there any friends or habits that would be potentially harmful to our marriages? As a man, I like to think that I would protect my wife from all intruders, and I would. But do I also protect my eyes and thoughts from intruders that might injure my marriage? Do I stop myself from looking at the "invaders" that would cause me to think of any woman other than my wife? It depends on how strong I am. It depends on how mature I am. No, it really depends on whether I understand what real love is. Love always protects!

Do I always trust? Trusting varies from person to person. Some spouses tend to smother the other with a lack of trust. Other spouses choose not to trust their marriage partner's opinions or ideas. The question boils down to, "Am I mature enough to count on the person I have chosen to become one flesh with?" Am I mature enough to let go and give her space rather than trying to own her like an object?

I always hope and always persevere. This is a key for every marriage. Things don't go as planned. Marriage brings many disappointments as well as many happy times. In order to make it through the disappointments, a decision must be made. I must decide always to hope that the future will bring a better relationship and to persevere toward that day. I need to do this. I can't count on my spouse to make the necessary changes to bring happiness to the marriage. My hope is in the Lord. I persevere with His power and strength (see Zech. 4:6b). This is His plan for marriage and love, so He must be willing to jump in and help if we are willing to hope and persevere for Christ's sake.

Love never fails. This is a hard look at love if we just focus on that other person. My spouse may fail, but my response toward that spouse can still be consistent. I may have to make some difficult decisions, but I can still maintain an attitude of choosing to love and wishing the best for my spouse.

All of this is a choice. It's also obviously not a feeling, but an action that we take toward another person. We decide to trust that the Author of love knows best, even if sometimes it seems so hard to love someone at this level.

Practice Doing Love

I think God knew that this very selfless kind of love would be difficult for us to know how to accomplish. He decided to give many of us a practice opportunity. At the birth of our first child, Torrey, I was ecstatic. My ecstasy was made even easier, if not obnoxious, by the fact that Torrey was an extremely beautiful baby right from the start.

That first day I remember standing at the window of the hospital nursery, looking at my baby amidst the twenty other newborns. It was amazing how her beauty stood out when she was next to those other ugly babies.

There was a father on my left, also looking in the window. He was talking to people, who were probably his in-laws, and saying, "Isn't she beautiful?" I realized that he was talking about my baby, so I turned to acknowledge that she was mine. But when I looked, I saw that he was looking at another baby. Looking down at the baby he was talking about, I saw a baby that was all wrinkled and disgusting. It looked like a little monkey! I couldn't believe he used the word *beautiful*.

Standing on the other side of me there was a man with a video camera. I figured he was from the local television station and had heard about my beautiful baby. But he was taking pictures of his newborn. When I looked over I saw a sight that certainly was not worth filming. It was a little baby with such an ugly head they had put a knit cap on it! It was baffling to me that those guys didn't feel somewhat jealous when they looked at their babies compared to mine. Mine was beautiful!

About a year later, I was looking in a drawer for something and found the picture that the hospital takes of your newborn and gives to each parent. Wow, had Torrey come a long way since that picture! She looked so bad in that picture that I couldn't believe it. Of course, now she is model material!

How is it that we deceive ourselves so much? How is it that I didn't realize that my baby was just as funny looking as everyone else's? It's a choice we make. Somehow, consciously or subconsciously, we choose to see our babies as beautiful and perfect.

In the Greek language, when they use the word *love*, they have several different words to help get a more exact meaning across. One of those words is *Eros*. Eros comes very close to our concept of romance. It's where we get our word *erotic*. It is a conditional love. I love you because of what you do for me. *Agape* is another word that the Greek language uses for love. This kind of love is just the opposite. It's the kind of love a parent has for a baby. That baby does nothing for the family, but they love it, even for its inability to do anything.

Eros love says that I love you because of all the things you do for me. I love you because you are beautiful and meet my needs. Agape says, "You are beautiful and very special to me simply because I love you. My love makes you special to me." This very same concept that we practice on a baby is the choice we need to make toward a spouse. Agape says that I choose to love, and that makes you beautiful to me. It's a choice, not a feeling.

Smelly Old Bear

Years ago I was reading Tony Campolo's book *It's Friday, but Sunday's Coming*. In it he comments on his child's stuffed animal and this whole concept of love. My own baby, Torrey, had a stuffed animal given to her by a very special friend of ours. Mary had purchased a little stuffed bear she found at a craft fair, and she gave it to us at Torrey's birth.

We put the little bear in Torrey's crib. Initially, she paid it no attention. Slowly, over time, this little bear became Torrey's most significant companion. She held that bear at night and during naps. During her first year and a half of life, Torrey sucked the bear's face off and ate both ears. Then she would stuff the remnants of the ears up her own nose. It was disgusting, and the bear began to smell. We constantly washed it, but it became obvious that if we continued to wash this smelly old bear we were going to find it in the washing machine lint trap. It was getting that decrepit.

One day, as I was walking through a mall while a craft fair was going on, I found another brand-new bear just like Torrey's smelly old bear. Only this bear was new and had a face and ears. I bought it, and couldn't wait to get home. Torrey was excited to have this new bear, so I hid her old one and waited for bedtime.

When Torrey got ready for bed (every mother reading this book already knows what happened), she looked up at me and said, "Where's Bear, Daddy." To which I responded, "Bear's gone on a trip, but now you have a new bear. And he smells good, too." Torrey dropped her new bear on the floor and said, "Oh no, Daddy! This is Other Bear! I want Bear!"

I was amazed. It didn't matter how badly that bear was worn out. It was hers and she loved it. They had been through much together. That bear had been with her when she was sick and when she was sad. She didn't want anything new, even if it was shaped more like the way a bear is supposed to be shaped. This was a child teaching her parents about agape love.

Our job is to choose to love each other. It's not a feeling. It's not even passion. Love is a choice that we make. It's an action that we choose to take toward that person we are loving. You aren't *in* love; you *do* love.

Torrey saw something in the smelly old bear that nobody else could see. My spouse must be beautiful and special and wonderful because I love her. Not the other way around. My love isn't dependent upon my spouse. It's dependent upon my maturity level. Love is a choice.

But the Smelly Old Bear Is Me

One night, as I was sitting in Torrey's bedroom, I noticed that the smelly old bear had fallen from her crib to the floor. I reached over to pick it up and held on to it for a moment. All at once I realized that, in God's hands, I am like that old bear. I like to think that I'm really something special, but in the greater scope of history, down deep inside I know I'm not anything special. But that's okay! God doesn't love me because I can do anything. He loves me with agape love. God loves me by choice.

He loves each of us so much that He sent His Son, Jesus Christ, to pay the price for the only thing that comes between me and God, my sin. Christ died on the cross as payment for my sin, and all I had to do was accept that action on my behalf. All I had to do was say, "Father, forgive me. I accept the fact that Christ died in my place." Then I am placing my life in His hands.

I may be a smelly old bear as far the universe is concerned, but the Creator of the universe counts me as very special when I'm in His hand. Not a smelly old bear, but a precious child of God. That, too, is a choice that we each must make. It's a choice that will impact everything else we do, especially our marriages.

When we have placed our lives in God's hand, God can empower us to love more maturely. He can empower us to forgive one another and provide the strength to grow in a deeper relationship. Christ is the key to a marriage that is filled with real love. "Dear friends, let us love one another, for love comes from God. Everyone who loves has been born of God and knows God" (1 John 4:7 NIV).